BLACK UNITED METHODISTS PREACH!

Black United Methodists Preach!

Edited by
Gennifer Benjamin Brooks

Abingdon Press
Nashville

BLACK UNITED METHODISTS PREACH!

This book is printed on acid-free paper.

Library of Congress Cataloging-in-Publication Data

ISBN 978-1-4267-4833-2

Cataloging-in-Publication data has been applied for with the Library of Congress.

All scripture quotations unless noted otherwise are taken from the New Revised Standard Version of the Bible, copyright 1989, Division of Christian Education of the National Council of the Churches of Christ in the United States of America. Used by permission. All rights reserved.

Scripture quotations marked NIV are taken from the Holy Bible, NEW INTERNATIONAL VERSION®. Copyright © 1973, 1978, 1984 by International Bible Society. All rights reserved throughout the world. Used by permission of International Bible Society.

Scripture quotations marked "NKJV™" are taken from the New King James Version®. Copyright © 1982 by Thomas Nelson, Inc. Used by permission. All rights reserved.

Scripture quotations from *THE MESSAGE*. Copyright © by Eugene H. Peterson 1993, 1994, 1995, 1996, 2000, 2001, 2002. Used by permission of NavPress Publishing Group.

Scripture quotations marked KJV are taken from the King James or Authorized Version of the Bible.

12 13 14 15 16 17 18 19 20 21—10 9 8 7 6 5 4 3 2 1

MANUFACTURED IN THE UNITED STATES OF AMERICA

In loving memory
of
Edsel A. Ammons
(1924–2010)

Acknowledgments

This book is dedicated to the late Bishop Edsel Albert Ammons, a gifted and inspiring preacher and shepherd leader of the church. A devout and devoted man of God, he served the church faithfully as pastor, teacher, and advocate for peace, justice, and unity among all people. He was a humble servant of Christ and the church, and his gentle spirit was often belied by his resounding pulpit voice. He held to a standard of excellence in his various roles of pastor, seminary professor, community advocate, and episcopal leader. He carried himself with dignity at all times and, through his life and work, shared his love of Jesus Christ with all people. He had a deep love for preaching and the ability to weave the words of his sermon into a poetic and grace-filled offering that invited hearers into an experiential engagement with Christ that was similar to his own. He believed that solid biblical preaching enhanced, emboldened, and empowered the ministry of Christ's church. His legacy lives on in the lives he touched.

Throughout all of life, there are persons who walk beside us. Some are there simply to cheer us on, and others join us in doing the things that help to make life joyful and our work pleasing. To these and all who consider themselves connected in any way with this work, I offer heartfelt thanks. I am deeply grateful to Bishop Edsel and Helen Ammons, with whom I first shared the idea and who encouraged me from the beginning to do this work. Heartfelt thanks go to my prayer partner Iris Green, who also became my typist; to my friend and sounding board Leo Curry; to Cherida Gary, who labored to do the work of transcribing the videos and editing the manuscripts; and to my family and all those friends and colleagues who continue to support my work. Above all, thanks to all the contributors who trusted me with their work, and especially

Bishop Gregory Palmer, who urged me to get the book done and then used his influence to enable its publication.

God's richest blessings to all.

Gennifer Benjamin Brooks
April 1, 2011

Contents

Contents

Foreword*

The opportunity to proclaim the gospel of Jesus Christ is a gift that every pastor should cherish always. Yet each should approach this grace-filled task with a sense of responsibility, with joy, and above all with humility. That God would give us such a magnificent gift of salvation through Jesus Christ and that we should be entrusted with the secret of the ages, through our connection to Christ and our commitment to ministry in his name, should make us humble. Preachers are called to be prophets in the oldest sense of the word. As prophets we are God's mouthpiece. We have been given the authority to speak for God to the people of God. We cannot and must not take lightly the great and wondrous love of God that first called us out and then gifted us with the ideas, words, and above all the Holy Spirit that alone gives life to what God has placed in our hearts and on our lips.

Preaching is intrinsic to the witness of the pastor. The pastor preaches with words and sometimes more clearly with the substance of her or his life. In its own way, the content of preaching arises as much from the song in our hearts as it does from the pages of scripture that we preach and the lives of the people to whom we offer the word of God's constant and never-ending love. Perhaps the idea of the sermon as song comes from the earliest years of my development in a musical household, where my mother and father were both pianists, although I did not follow them into the world

---

* This foreword containing the thoughts and words of Bishop Edsel A. Ammons was written by the editor from interviews and conversations with Bishop Ammons before his passing on December 24, 2010, and was approved by his wife, Mrs. Helen Ammons, who was present during the interviews and subsequent conversations.

of music as my brother did when he became a tenor saxophonist. The songs that played in my heart—that stirred the first real spark of self-awareness—came from the church, also an influential part of my early life and development.

Others saw in me what I was to later become, a preacher of the gospel, and at times I strained to hear the song that had charmed my spirit amidst the struggle for self-identification, self-determination, and Christian formation that marked my early adult years. My appointment to a small African American congregation, which was presented as a gift of grace while I tried to find my way to answer God's call, offered me the opportunity to preach to my small congregation each week. And despite my full work schedule, I appreciated the gift of divine grace, so I strove diligently each week to offer the people of God a word from the Lord. I'm sure that those early sermons left out much in the way of biblical interpretation and theological erudition, but they were offered humbly after due diligence and time spent with the text. And of course they and I depended fully on the grace of God to enable them to infect the hearts of God's people in that place.

My life as a preacher, whether as pastor of a local congregation or as a general superintendent and episcopal leader of many congregations, has been guided and directed by my love for God, my reverence for the word of God as found in the Scriptures, and my witness to the grace of God in my life and indeed in all of life. The joy of the Lord is indeed my strength, and the strength of my life comes from my faith in the eternal love of God. The substance of my sermons went beyond joy and faith. In developing each sermon, I approached the task with full knowledge of my weakness and my inability to offer anything worth hearing but that which had been placed in me by the Holy Spirit. At all times I labored to keep a sense of humility that I, even I, should be considered a fit vessel to speak for God.

The experience was contrary to what I had felt in the early days of accepting my call to ministry. I had not felt fit; in fact I believed myself too flawed to be of service to Christ's church. Yet here I was, daring to open my mouth sufficiently for God to fill it with good things. Perhaps it was that total dependence on God combined with the knowledge of my inabilities that enabled me to be a preacher of the gospel. Certainly I took little credit for the accolades that accompanied my preaching, but remembered always to give the praise and thanks to God for God's gracious gift. And my prayer was always that the words of my mouth would be acceptable to God and help guide some lost soul to the cross and the empty tomb.

Whether preaching to the laity in the local congregations or preaching to clergy in their gatherings or to both clergy and laity at annual conferences, my theology and my journey were the same. The sermon needed to be the word of God for the people of God. The message was ever the gospel of our Lord. And the purpose was always to offer a life-giving, life-shaping, transforming word that would enable the hearers to see again the Christ of their salvation and once again offer their lives to his service. My witness as a preacher is that my sermons pointed always to Christ and away from myself, allowing hearts to be opened to receive again God's amazing grace for their lives now and in the eternal future. Theologically, God in all three persons was present with me in the whole exercise of sermon development and proclamation: the selection of the text, the theme of the sermon, the determination of a title, the focus of the message, and every moment of delivery. There was no sermon without the divine presence. Without God, and certainly without the help of the Holy Spirit, there was no sermon worth preaching and no message worth delivering.

As my work in the church intensified and I began to send preachers into the field, my prayer was that they too would hold in tandem the joy of being called by God to speak for God and the humility to give God the credit for every message that they delivered to the people of God. My sorrow at hearing pastors who missed this understanding of the task of preaching was always accompanied by a prayer for the preachers' awakening to that understanding of their ministerial task. At times there were those whose message was lost in the clutter of their own ego and who went so far off the mark in preaching that no one could hear anything but idle chatter. Then my prayer was that the preacher would allow the Holy Spirit to silence the noise and open his or her ears and heart and mind to receive again the call to serve as one of God's prophets.

Within The United Methodist Church there are, thankfully, many who have followed not simply in the path of its founder, John Wesley, himself a preacher of the word of God, but in the pathway of the saints and prophets long gone who remind us that the words we speak must become always the word of God for the people of God. The Black church has always been acclaimed for its preaching. Its dependence on scripture and its emotive emphasis have been cornerstones of a preaching style that has engendered hope, called to faith, and wrestled joy out of despair for generations of people. Great preaching has never been a unilateral accomplishment of all Black preachers; and Black United Methodist preachers, as members of an essentially White denomination, have not been recognized generally for their preaching, except for a small number of individual cases. This book offers a small sampling of Black United Methodist preachers and offers to the whole church an understanding, admittedly limited in scope, of what makes for good preaching.

Dr. Brooks, a teacher of preachers and herself an accomplished preacher, in her selection of preachers across the United Methodist connection, offers a glimpse into a wide range of sermon styles and provides an opportunity for us to listen in as these preachers prepare and offer a word for God. The preachers and the sermons remind us that there is a multiplicity of styles in preaching and that it is not the style, nor even the delivery, but the preacher's understanding of the nature of preaching as proclamation of the gospel that makes for effective or even great preaching.

My hope for this book is that the conversations of the preachers, each sharing her or his sermonic process and theology of preaching, and the sermons that they have produced may help lead other struggling preachers to find their way to becoming faithful prophets who speak only God's word. I am grateful that our electronic age will provide an opportunity for you to hear each sermon in the preacher's voice as it was preached. Sermons are for hearing and not simply for reading. My own ministry of preaching has come to an end, but my ears and heart are open always as I listen to the sermons of other preachers so that, even in these late years of my life, I may again hear a word of God's magnificent and eternal grace, offered to me for the continuous transformation of my life. And by that divine grace may I be led again to commit myself—heart, soul, and body—to the will of God, and claim for myself the cross and the resurrection of my savior Jesus Christ for my life now and in eternity.

May it be so through Jesus Christ.

Edsel A. Ammons

Introduction

Black people have been a part of the Methodist Church in America from its inception.[1] William B. McClain's landmark work about Black Methodists records the attendance at the first meeting of the John Street Society of New York City. "Among the first worshippers was Betty, a black servant of the Heck household."[2] Not only were they members of the fledgling movement, but Black people were also part of the preaching ministry of the church early in the development of American Methodism, as noted in *The United Methodist Book of Discipline*. Two notable African American preachers, Harry Hosier and Richard Allen, are believed to have been present at the famous Christmas Conference of preachers that was held in Baltimore in December 1784.[3] And as the Second Great Awakening sped across the landscape of American Protestantism during the early part of the nineteenth century, Black preachers played an active role in the revivals and camp meetings.

As Methodism continued to develop in America, Black people, slaves for the most part, continued to be drawn to the evangelistic style of the preachers, mainly, as McClain notes, because "the black slaves heard of a good loving God who knew the sufferings of his children, even his sun-baked sons and daughters who found themselves in chains in a strange land."[4] The simple, even simplistic message of good news for all people was one that caught the burdened hearts of Black people in America, and their attraction to the message moved many of their numbers, both male and female, to move beyond hearing to proclamation of the good news of divine love. Beyond the attraction of the message, Black people remained drawn to Methodism because of the Methodist stance against slavery and also because they were permitted to be part of the leadership of the societies as preachers of the gospel.

Black Methodist preachers followed their White counterparts in their evangelistic style of preaching. They were all concerned with conversion and were dramatic in the presentation of the message in order to appeal to the emotions and move the hearers to ecstatic renunciation of sin and acceptance of Christ.

> These preachers' style was dictated both by the message and an overriding passionate goal: to help the poor sinner make a decision for heaven rather than allow their souls to be consigned to hell. And the preachers exhorted this fiery message of salvation and hope with personal appeal, and enthusiasm that often triggered responses of infectious groans and shouts which spread throughout the meeting place.[5]

The exuberant style of Methodist preaching appealed both to the cultural roots of their African ancestry and to the hope of freedom to which they held desperately in the midst of the inhuman oppression of slavery. The preachers who arose from their midst, despite their inability to read, ably delivered stirring messages of salvation and hope. One such preacher, Harry Hosier, although illiterate, became such a notable preacher that, after he preached in one of their congregations, a suggestion was put forward that he might be useful in helping restore the zeal of New York congregants.[6]

The evangelistic, exuberant, emotive style of preaching that developed among Methodist preachers continued to be passed down through generations of Black preachers and has come to be associated mainly with Black preaching. But perhaps as important as the style of preaching was the role of the preacher in the community. During slavery, Black preachers played an important leadership role in the community and were afforded great respect by the congregation. This may have helped fuel the splits that came in the Methodist Episcopal Church as Black people continued to experience a lack of respect from White congregations. Black preachers and congregants in general were expected to maintain the subservient role in White congregations that they were forced to endure during slavery and beyond it into the Jim Crow era. Black preachers, the leaders of the community, were moved in their demand for true Christian treatment, to gather their people and walk away from congregations that denied them full personhood. This did not mean, however, that they walked away from

Methodism. Instead, claiming their African identity, Black preachers created new denominations that claimed both the Methodist and the African heritage. Other Black denominations developed outside Methodism, and the tradition of Black preaching as vibrant, emotive, and effective in winning souls to Christ continued to be regarded and respected among Protestant circles.

Methodist Episcopal congregations where Blacks continued to hold membership, similar to the society in which they lived, were subjected to the challenge of race and gave in to the call for segregation between Whites and Blacks. The Central Jurisdiction, created in 1939 at the uniting conference of The Methodist Church, was Methodism's way of solving the dilemma of Blacks in The Methodist Church.[7] What this accomplished, in effect, was the creation of a Black denomination within a White denomination. In doing so, the tradition of Black preaching was carried forward. For those Blacks left behind, those persons who were small minorities within White congregations or the very few predominantly Black congregations that were not part of the Central Jurisdiction, the legacy of Black preaching was muted if not lost. In part because of their assimilation into the culture of White and generally middle-class congregations, Blacks became accustomed to and even adopted a more cerebral and less emotive style of preaching. With the dissolution of the Central Jurisdiction in 1964 and the creation of The United Methodist Church in 1968, its minority Black constituents were considered by some, especially in the Black denominations, to have lost their preaching voice.

The creation of Black Methodists for Church Renewal (BMCR), the official Black caucus of The United Methodist Church, was intended to ensure that the voices of Black people were not lost in the myriad voices of the newly merged church. While BMCR did help mitigate the possibility of de facto segregation in the leadership of the new church, what it did not do was provide assurance to Black denominations that the legacy of Black preaching would remain a part of the basically White denomination. As a result, although there are many Black preachers within The United Methodist Church who have been lauded for their preaching and a few individual preachers have been singled out for special recognition, generally, Black preachers in United Methodism are not considered purveyors of the evangelistic, emotive, and even exuberant style that is considered authentic Black preaching.

Homiletics scholar Henry Mitchell, in his book *Black Preaching*, notes that Martin Luther King Sr. once declared from the pulpit of the Ebenezer Baptist Church of Atlanta that there was no such thing as Black preaching,[8] but Cleo La Rue in *The Heart of Black Preaching* names a few elements that some persons have considered distinctive to Black preaching. "Some have pointed to the high place of scripture in the African American tradition, others to the black preacher's creative use of language and storytelling, and still others to the free play of emotion and celebration in the preaching event or to communication techniques such as call-and-response."[9] However, La Rue also notes correctly that although all the elements noted with respect to Black preaching are correctly identified, they are not unique to the African American context and in fact can be found to some degree outside of the Black tradition.

As stated earlier, these same elements were present in the evangelistic style of early Methodist preachers, especially during the revivals and camp meetings of the early to mid-nineteenth century. One might be justified in saying that Black preachers in The United Methodist Church have a dual source for their own strain of Black preaching. Certainly the evangelism of early Methodism and its emphasis on conversion and salvation through the grace of God, a Methodist tenet, remains foundational to Black preaching across the Christian Church, including The United Methodist Church. Frank Thomas considers Black preaching to be fundamentally "about helping people experience the assurance of grace that is the gospel."[10] The use of scripture to proclaim the gospel message is a key attribute of Black preaching, which is meant always to offer hope for a better life, to a culture of people who often experience a sense of hopelessness because of the disproportionate challenges to life that they face in society.

The tradition of preaching hope follows from the messages preached to the slaves of early Methodism that encouraged the celebration of their personhood, which was denied by society, and called forth the emotional involvement of preachers and hearers. Thomas stresses that to be authentic, Black preachers are called to make a deliberate appeal to the emotions through their sermons.[11] Dependence on scripture, a sense of hope, emotional appeal, and celebration are thus key elements of Black preaching. It is a journey that requires the preacher, empowered by the Holy Spirit, to come holistically to the task of preaching in order to help hearers give themselves totally to God in their conversion. Both Mitchell and Thomas consider Black preaching as celebrative.[12] The necessity for appealing to the emotion in preaching does not negate the need for sermons to be cognitive and intuitive as well as emotive. As Thomas expounds, "[I]f the preacher would utilize emotional context and process in the preaching event, then the sermon must appeal to core belief."[13] Unfortunately, there are those within and outside of the Black community who consider Black preaching to be concerned mainly or even only with exciting the emotions and thus are misled into ignoring its cognitive appeal to reason and rationality and its intuitive appeal that can move people beyond reason or emotion to receive the evangelistic message of the gospel.

The United Methodist Church has become, to an extent that would be distressing to its founder, John Wesley, a church of the middle class. Even among Black congregations, the evangelistic fervor of the early years is seldom seen; however, that does not negate the fact that Black preaching is still a reality among the Black congregations of The United Methodist Church. The purpose of this book is to make that reality available across the connection and outside to the wider Christian church. Black preaching is part and parcel of the legacy and the current reality of The United Methodist Church. Many Black preachers in The United Methodist Church have maintained the standard of Black preaching to their congregations, and even those who serve outside regular congregational settings follow the model of Black preaching that calls souls to Christ and seeks justice for the oppressed.

This book showcases fourteen Black United Methodist preachers who are active in ministry across the connection. The list is deliberately representative of clergy who are ordained to preach the word of God. This does not deny the place of lay preachers, who have been a part of Methodism from the beginning; instead, it is meant to show the way in which the legacy of Black preaching has been carried forward by those who have covenanted to the preaching ministry of the church by their ordination. The list includes pastors of local congregations, episcopal leaders, district superintendents, and persons engaged in the conference and general agencies of the church. As the title proclaims, they are all Black United Methodists who preach.

In each chapter, the preacher discusses the factors that influence him or her in the task of developing and preaching the sermon. This may include theology of preaching, process of sermon preparation, criteria for selecting texts or topics for preaching, use of scripture, contextual concerns, the influence of society and culture, the issue of justice, and other influences that have helped shape them as preachers of the gospel. In addition, the chapter will include the full manuscript of a sermon he or she has preached. A concluding chapter will summarize the goal of preaching in the church and will include a final sermon by the editor that pays tribute to Bishop Ammons.

Since I believe that sermons are experienced fully as they are heard and not read, the preached sermons will be available for viewing online on the Styberg Preaching Institute page on the Garrett-Evangelical Theological Seminary website (www.garrett.edu) through the link provided in the footnote on the first page of each sermon.

Notes

1. I use the term *Black* in order to be inclusive of all people of color who trace their origins from native people of the continent of Africa.

2. William B. McClain, *Black People in the Methodist Church: Whither Thou Goest* (Nashville: Abingdon Press, 1984), 17.

3. See "Historical Statement" in *The Book of Discipline of The United Methodist Church* (Nashville: The United Methodist Publishing House, 2000), 11.

4. McClain, *Black People in the Methodist Church,* 19.

5. Ibid., 27.

6. Ibid., 44.

7. See James S. Thomas, *Methodism's Racial Dilemma: The Story of the Central Jurisdiction* (Nashville: Abingdon Press, 1992), which offers a comprehensive history of the Central Jurisdiction.

8. Henry Mitchell, *Black Preaching* (New York: Harper & Row, 1970), 11.

9. Cleophus J. La Rue, *The Heart of Black Preaching* (Louisville: Westminster John Knox Press, 2000), 1.

10. Frank A. Thomas, *They Like to Never Quit Praisin' God: The Role of Celebration in Preaching* (Cleveland: Pilgrim Press, 1997), 3.

11. Ibid., 4.

12. Henry H. Mitchell expounds this claim in his book *Celebration & Experience in Preaching* (Nashville: Abingdon Press, 1990), and Frank A. Thomas follows Mitchell, his teacher, in his treatment of celebration in preaching in his text referenced earlier.

13. Thomas, *They Like to Never Quit Praisin' God,* 8.

Contributors

Rose Booker-Jones is pastor of Bethel United Methodist Church, Peoria, Illinois.

Leo W. Curry is pastor of Fordham United Methodist Church, Bronx, New York.

Safiyah Fosua is director of transformational preaching at the General Board of Discipleship.

Telley Lynnette Gadson is pastor of Saint Mark United Methodist Church, Sumter, South Carolina.

Gennifer Benjamin Brooks is the Ernest and Bernice Styberg Associate Professor of Homiletics and Director of the Styberg Preaching Institute at Garrett-Evangelical Theological Seminary. She is an elder in the New York Conference.

Linda Lee is bishop of the Wisconsin Area.

Pamela Lightsey is Associate Dean of Community Life and Lifelong Learning and Clinical Assistant Professor of Contextual Theology and Practice at Boston University School of Theology.

Okitakoyi Lundula, originally from the Democratic Republic of Congo, is pastor of Nashua United Methodist Church and the Republic Community Church in the Iowa Conference.

Tracy Smith Malone is superintendent of the Southern District in the Northern Illinois Conference.

Gregory Palmer is bishop of the Illinois Great Rivers Conference.

Vance P. Ross is pastor of Gordon Memorial United Methodist Church in Nashville, Tennessee.

Robert O. Simpson is pastor of Janes United Methodist Church, Brooklyn, New York.

Rodney T. Smothers is pastor of the St. Paul-Corkran Memorial Cooperative Parish in Oxon Hill and Temple Hills, Maryland, and congregational consultant and leadership coach.

James E. Swanson, Sr., is bishop of the Knoxville Area.

Dorothy Watson-Tatem is superintendent of the East District in the Eastern Pennsylvania Conference.

CHAPTER ONE

An Encounter with God

Linda Lee

God speaks to humanity through the Holy Scriptures, through the stories and teachings they offer. When I first began to preach, I understood myself to be the vessel through which God spoke because I had only spoken publically during church programs and didn't really like speaking in public. But God guides us through the challenges and celebrations of the human experience, and by revealing truths about myself and my experiences God inspires my faith and enables understanding that provides the capacity to deal with challenges, obstacles, and dangers.

From my first experience of preaching I came to the realization that this was God's call on my life, but it took many years of preaching and pastoring before I accepted that I was indeed called to preach. In the early years of preaching, my confidence in my sermons came from the knowledge that I was seminary trained and thus had the right interpretation of the Scriptures. The fact that the people in my congregation just weren't "getting" what I was preaching to them was frustrating, and it took a conversation with God for me to come to an understanding of the context of the people to whom I was preaching and the importance of not only understanding their context but also understanding that I was part of that context—namely, sinners saved by God's grace. That understanding has remained with me throughout my years of preaching, and it enables me to share openly and willingly my witness, experience, and understanding of God.

Each setting of preaching offers a unique encounter with God. Preaching is an organism of the Holy Spirit that is never again duplicated and thus a unique and singular expression of God's presence. The proclamation of good news is my public witness—a sharing of my personal experience with God through events of healing, family challenges, and other life crises. And the purpose of that public witness, as well as the witness of scripture, is to assist people in becoming acquainted with God and in developing the capacity to experience personally a transformative encounter with the living God in our midst. Whether I am guided by the lectionary or I'm asked to preach a specific text or topic or I preach from a text of my choice, my most important criterion for engaging the task of preaching is prayer. I ask God to reveal to me the word God has for the people to whom God is sending me. I pray also that God will reveal to me the specific word for me; because without that word, I have nothing to offer.

Reading the text and exploring what was going on in its biblical context allows a key metaphor to emerge, which is the start of the writing process. Whether following my normal practice of using a manuscript or being guided by an outline, I've learned to trust God to enable me to preach the message that is appropriate to the particular congregation. I work diligently to discover the social realities, the human condition, or the need that may be present in the text in order to discern the parallels and apply them to the present context. There is a consistency both to human nature and to God's nature, and this work of discovery brings to light the constancy of God's love and presence as a mitigating force for human behavior.

It is important for me as preacher to discover more of the nature and Spirit of God within us in order to reveal to the hearers the indwelling Christ. For twenty-first-century Christians, there continues to be the need for voices that call for counter-cultural practices that defy violence, domination, greed, and unholy living. I am committed to be a voice that speaks peace and justice for all people; that dedication helps energize my delivery whether from behind the pulpit or moving around the pulpit area or walking to each part of the sanctuary in the midst of the people. Through the anointing of the Holy Spirit, I become an instrument through which God speaks peace and calls for justice for all people.

The animated, energetic, and enthusiastic style of my preaching is meant to invite hearers into the experience I'm having with God. At times, my focus is on teaching, which is less animated; but in every case my hope is to accomplish what the Lord has sent me to do, to say what God has given me to say, remembering always that it's not about what I feel or don't feel. God can and will use me (or any of us) in God's way. So I need to be "prayed up" and available to the Holy Spirit in the preaching moment so that God's word will go forth through the words I speak, but in the power of the Holy Spirit. Only so will people experience the presence and the power of God, which will enable them to leave different and better people than they were when they arrived.

Over the years, listening to some of my favorite preachers, such as Bishop John Bryant, Dr. Samuel Proctor, Bishop Leontyne T. C. Kelly, Dr. Charles Adams, and Dr. Jeremiah Wright, I've attempted to learn some technique, style, or skill from each of them. But learning how to be fully myself and fully available to God in the preaching moment, as well as the importance of good research, written and spiritual preparation, and good contemporary application, are the most important lessons I learned from these great orators.

What I love best about preaching is the ways I encounter God. God preaches to me in the preparation, in scripture, through the Holy Spirit in the preaching moment; in the souls that are touched and sometimes healed or helped by the word. God has given me a testimony that has voice in my sermons as I continue my walk with Jesus Christ. Regardless of the challenges of life, I've learned to tell the story. That story is the good news that God really does love us, and that Jesus is a living Savior who epitomizes God's love, who lives and moves and loves among the people of God.

Choose Life[*]
Deuteronomy 30:15-20

Moses and the Hebrews had left the land and life of enslavement. Their departure was just the beginning of two generations of victory and challenge as they found their way to the precipice of the land promised to their ancestors. God's hand had guided them this far, providing signs and wonders from the instant Moses accepted God's call to lead them to this very time in the life and history of their people. Two generations had died out and now those who had survived the wilderness, the grandchildren of the ones who left Egypt, were about to enter and live into the promise God had made decades before.

For forty years, Moses had been a steadfast and faithful guide and *now* even he had to let go. But having given his life and all of himself to this call, everything within him needed for those who would carry on to do so through the same source of power and help and support and love that he had come to know and trust and love. Building a new nation could not be accomplished by human effort alone. No amount of law or political machinations or planning would enable them to accomplish what was before them. They were going to need complete clarity about where their power and their help were coming from. Moses knew and wanted them to understand that the help and power they needed to take them forward could come only from God.

Now it should not have been difficult for this generation to recognize the truth of what Moses was trying to tell them. Miracles had become normal for them. As they grew up, they had seen a rod turn into a snake, bitter water become sweet, and manna fall from heaven, with every day bringing just the amount that was needed. But this generation would need to remember they had a choice. When taking possession of the promised land got ugly, when death and destruction was a stench in the nostrils, when grief and fear and anger and weariness threatened to overcome their ability to complete the task at hand, they needed to remember that they had a choice. And that they must choose life.

* This sermon was preached in celebration of Black History Month in the Chapel of the Unnamed Faithful of Garrett-Evangelical Theological Seminary in Evanston, Illinois, on February 8, 2011. View the preaching of this sermon on www.garrett.edu/styberg-bump/lee

And when things got real good and the pleasures of life got real enjoyable and everybody had a job and enough food to eat and wine to drink and a nice home to live in and furniture and a beautiful wife and a handsome husband and gorgeous, talented, well-mannered children—they would have to choose then too. Choose not to be seduced by too much of any good thing—choose not to let the good things become god to them and take the place of the God of their ancestors. It was essential for the generation going forward to understand how important it was for them to remember they had a choice. And that they must choose life.

What does it mean for people of African descent in the United States to choose life in the twenty-first century? Like the Hebrews in Egypt, Africans in the Diaspora of the U.S. continue to experience brutal oppression, marginalization, demoralization, and exclusion. In the midst of corporations, institutions—including the church—and local and national government, racism continues daily to impact the mental, physical, and spiritual health of people of African descent in measurable and immeasurable ways.

The condition of many of our communities and congregations, and the suffering and struggle of so many of our people, are not unlike the plight of the Hebrews standing with Pharaoh's army threatening sure annihilation behind them and the certain death of the Red Sea in front of them. They had nowhere to turn, no place to run, and no place to hide. There was no hope of escape back into the past and no possibility of moving forward into a new future. But in that moment God moved! And made a way where there seemed to be no other way forward.

Consider some of our communities today, where all the supermarkets have fled and left single mothers and parents with young children in need of healthy nourishment. Day after day they are ripped off financially and health-wise because they have no choice but to feed their families with overpriced, old, canned, denatured food from what we used to call the mom and pop stores that are all that are left in the neighborhood. Where else can they go without a car or money for both a cab and food or without the time and energy to take a bus to the suburbs—if there is a bus? Consider the plethora of violence in music, video games, TV, and movies. Gang life, domestic violence, and verbal and emotional abuse plague our communities and even some of our congregations. Consider the prevalence of drugs and alcohol in African American and other communities of color. Who makes them available and why? And every time the current President of the U.S., a man who happens to have Black blood running through his veins, is attacked and maligned and insulted and disrespected, every person of African descent in this nation is impacted, whether they are consciously aware of it or not. Where are our children to go to see that there are other ways we can treat each other—life-giving, life-affirming ways? What will enable them to choose life?

But just like God opened the Red Sea for the Hebrew children in the Old Testament, God has intervened for people of African descent in the U.S. over and over and over again, through the efforts of saints in our midst who, like Moses, have been called to give their lives for the sake of the community. People like my friend Sherri, who has given her life as a therapist, working only in places where people of African descent with most need of her services can get them. She has worked for less money and less personal stability in order to serve God's people who otherwise would not have the support to build new lives. God opens the Red Sea in front of us and overcomes Pharaoh's army behind us every day through those, some in this very room, who open possibility and accessibility to the men, women, and children otherwise left to suffer or die. We have had times of wandering in the wilderness since the Civil Rights Movement of the late 1950s and early 1960s. Now some of the generation who led us out of the legal segregation, social marginalization, and spiritual pain of that era are dying out. But we are on the precipice today of entering a promised land, of building a new nation of healthy, self-aware, gifted, confident, creative, spiritually grounded, faith-filled people who know what it means to choose life.

In spite of all the protestations and so-called research and posturing about African American people being less intelligent, more lazy, more prone to violence, sexually preoccupied and promiscuous, and all the other misrepresentations made up by those who have a need to do so, we continue to set the standard. We are imitated in popular vernacular, clothing style, walk, hair styles, even beauty. Folk still want thick lips and full hips while demeaning the dark skin and nappy hair that naturally accompany them. But we also set the standard for spiritual and ethical character. Dr. Joy

Degruy, in her book *Post Traumatic Slave Syndrome,* writes: "We have demonstrated time and time again that we can courageously fight for justice, we are not crippled with hatred or rage....We are strong, resilient, industrious, creative, forgiving....We are a spiritual, loving, hopeful people."[1] Through it all, we choose life.

We choose life because we have hope; because we know that God still makes a way out of no way. God has a bigger plan than we can see; a plan for people of African descent; a part for us to play in the grand scheme of things; a plan not just for us and ours. God's thoughts are higher than our thoughts. God's ways are higher than our ways. God's plans for all of humanity are for good and not for harm—to give the whole human race a future with hope. The land and territory God promised is spread before us. It is a vast panorama of possibility and opportunity. Our task, our challenge and the thing we must do today, is to remember that we have a choice. We can choose blessing and life or we can choose curses and death. God's promise to us and to all of humanity in and through Jesus Christ is not a physical territory, but it is real just the same. The land Jesus promises us is a territory within us that when we have possessed it overflows into family and community, congregation and world. We have the capacity to be renewed, rebuilt, and revived, beginning with the transformation of our minds. Whatever the challenges and obstacles we may be facing— as individuals, as congregations, as communities—we have a choice.

We can choose life! Jesus said, I am the way, the truth, and the life. Whoever believes in me, though they die, they will yet live. Jesus said, I have come that they may have life and have it abundantly.

What does it mean to choose life? Our ancestors chose life. In antiquity, long before the Atlantic slave trade, they chose life through living the values of Maat—truth, justice, reciprocity, rightness, and balance. Oba T'Shaka, in his book *Return to the African Mother Principle of Male and Female Equality,* wrote: "Just as a male or female must demonstrate the spiritual, mental and physical attributes of honesty, justice, bravery, respect, and hard work before they could enjoy the rights of manhood or womanhood, so the King [or queen—my addition] must display through the highest qualities of responsible, ethical conduct, these same character traits."[2] Choosing life for them was not theory; it was a practice.

During the Middle Passage our captured ancestors chose life even when death was the reasonable antidote to the horror and inhuman terrorism that staying alive promised. They chose life all during the years of brutality and abuse of chattel slavery and every effort that was made to prove that it was they who had lost their humanity. We carry the DNA of those who understood what it means to choose life. And our text for today defines it with three actions. To choose life means first, to love God, second, to obey God, and third, to hold on to God.

Once, in the eyes of some, we were not a people, but now we are God's people. Once, even in our own eyes we may have received no mercy, but now we know God's mercy. We are a chosen race, a royal priesthood, a holy nation! Not for the purpose of dominating others or puffing ourselves up. God chooses us to be among the witnesses who proclaim the mighty acts of the One who calls all races, all peoples, all nations, out of darkness into God's marvelous light! How can we help but love God with all our heart, all our mind, all our soul, and all our being, and our neighbor and ourselves?

And if we love God, how can we help but obey God? Our mamas and grandmas and some of our daddies and grandpas showed us how. They taught us the importance of obedience. Sometimes it was with a belt or a switch. But they knew obedience could be a matter of life and death. So we learned what it meant to obey. When I was a young mother, my sons were playing outside one sunny summer day. It was quiet; it was peaceful; it was a beautiful day. Something told me to go and tell them to come in. It didn't make sense, I could see them and hear them, and they were fine. But something compelled me to make them come inside. So I did, with much fussing and disappointment from them. Within five minutes of the time they were both safely in the house, a man swerved around the corner in a pickup truck, and ran up onto the sidewalk and over the front yard where my sons had just been playing. All I could do was praise God for that word, that urging, that insistence. Because I was obedient my children were spared harm and possibly death.

Our mothers and fathers knew what it meant to obey God. It was God that kept them alive with a portion of their right mind and enough health and strength to just keep living and not die during the days of chattel slavery in the U.S. It was God who brought them safely across the swamps and fields of the Underground Railroad. It was God that guided them through the Jim Crow years of unjust murder of mainly successful black businessmen as a lesson to others uppity enough to think it was a goal they should aspire to. W. E. B. DuBois, Fannie Lou Hamer, Frederick Douglas, Sojourner Truth, Bishop James Thomas, Bishop Edsel Ammons, and many others left us a legacy—a legacy of choosing life. God continues to make a way, guiding us as we navigate the rough waters of the twenty-first century to choose life.

We can choose life because we know what it means to hold on to God. When Lazarus died Jesus waited before he went to be with the family. The disciples didn't understand. Mary and Martha didn't understand. But Jesus knew what he was doing. When he finally got there Lazarus had been in the tomb for four days. He was dead. He was stinking. There was no hope of anyone ever seeing him alive again. But Jesus had waited until then so he could prove what happens when we hold on to God. When hope is past, gone, no longer on the radar screen, that's the very time we must hold on to God. Jesus said, Lazarus, come out! Lazarus, get up! Lazarus, choose life! And Lazarus's soul chose life. Lazarus's heart chose life. Lazarus's body chose life. While he was still in the tomb he breathed in the breath of life once more. While he was still in the tomb he started moving his fingers and his toes. While he was still in the tomb he opened his eyes to see again. While he was still in the tomb he got up and at the sound of the master's voice he came out. He could hear his Savior calling, he could hear his Savior calling, he could hear his Savior calling, "Come and follow, follow me."

No matter what external conditions we face as a people, as a congregation, as a nation, as a world, we have a choice. God has set before us today life and death, blessings and curses. Let us choose life, let us choose to love God with all our heart and mind and soul and strength, and our neighbors as ourselves. Let us choose life, to plant seeds of hope and build up faith, even the faith of obedience, seeking God's kingdom. Let us choose life by holding on to God's unchanging hand until the day that every tear is wiped from human eyes and death is no more, mourning and crying and pain are no more, and the new heaven and the new earth have come! We can choose life because we serve a Savior who is the way, the truth, and the life. "You ask me how I [we] know he lives? He lives within my [our] heart."

My sisters and brothers, choose life!

Notes

1. Joy Degruy Leary, *Post Traumatic Slave Syndrome* (Milwaukie, Ore.: Uptone Press, 2005), 188-89.

2. Oba T'Shaka, *Return to the African Mother Principle of Male and Female Equality* (Salem, Mass.: Pyramid Books, 1995), 41.

CHAPTER TWO

Led by the Spirit

Okitakoyi Lundula

Preaching is God's gift to the people and the church. I consider the church, wherever it is, to be the family of God, and I am always excited to share the word of God with the people of God through the ministry of preaching. I preach not because I want to but because I am called to preach by God. I feel empowered by God to preach the good news of our Lord and Savior Jesus Christ to the people of God, and my theology of preaching is based on faithfulness and obedience to the Spirit of God. I see myself as a simple tool that is being used by God to communicate God's will to the people of God.

I was already involved in the preaching ministry before I went to seminary. My time at the seminary helped me understand several aspects of the sermon development and the ministry of preaching. From my personal experience, through the ministry of preaching I have learned how to listen to God and deliver the word of God based on the context and location. My concern and challenge in preaching is delivering sermons that relate correctly to the church or community where the sermon is preached. I had and I continue to have a strong passion to preach the gospel to the people of God. Each community or each family of God has its own identity, realities, and problems. The word of God comes through a sermon as a response to the need of a particular community and at a particular time, so it is important to me that my sermon relate to the cultural context, the time, and the geographical location.

As I mentioned earlier, preaching is God's gift. A preacher is an instrument of God, gifted by God to proclaim divine grace through the interpretation of the gospel to the people of God. As preacher I must be empowered by God's Spirit to be God's mouthpiece to the people of God. The message delivered through the sermon has to change the life of the listeners; the spoken word has to bring hope to those who are hopeless, healing to those with broken hearts, light to those who are still in the darkness, courage to those who are discouraged, and assurance of salvation to all the people of

God. This is what makes a sermon become good news to the people of God. The preacher has to learn how to listen to God's Spirit and discern the will of God as the sermon is delivered to the particular community or church.

As a spiritual leader, I believe that the Scriptures are the word of God. The Second Letter to Timothy states, "All scripture is inspired by God and is useful for teaching, for reproof, for correction, and for training in righteousness, so that everyone who belongs to God may be proficient, equipped for every good work" (2 Timothy 3:16-17). Partly because of that belief, I follow the lectionary, even when the selected texts are challenging. I also select scriptures to preach based on a situation, event, or specific challenge facing the church or the community. In most cases, I will preach an expository sermon. I find that it gives me and the listeners the opportunity to dig deeply into one text and understand it. It also gives us the opportunity to have one focus that can be well understood and digested by the people of God.

I have developed a step-by-step process that I use to prepare my sermons. It begins and ends with prayer. I always start by asking for God's guidance to prepare a "meal" that will be appropriate to the people of God to whom I will be preaching. What follows is a careful reading of the biblical text in order to find the good news and interpret the text. This helps determine the shape of the sermon, and by using biblical commentaries and other resources, I am led to the message that will be the heart of the sermon. Once it is written to my satisfaction, I practice preaching the sermon and pray for myself and the listeners.

I was raised in the culture where the sermon would last at least forty to forty-five minutes, and that was normal and acceptable in that particular context. Today I serve congregations where the sermon has to last about ten to fifteen minutes. Each community of people has its own tradition and culture, and as a preacher I am very sensitive to the context of my sermons. I feel called to preach a word that promotes peace and love and builds strong relationship and mutual respect regardless of our geographical or educational background, and of our racial or language differences.

My concern in preaching is to reach the people where they are in that moment, not to make sure that I say all the words that I wrote. So, although I am careful in selecting the words of the sermon, I do not feel obligated to read my manuscript word for word. I take the written sermon into the pulpit and make sure it is open while I am preaching, since it provides a sense of security, but while preaching I work diligently to try to connect with the members of the congregation, even when they are not familiar to me.

I am comfortable preaching to the congregations where I am appointed, but preaching to an audience that I do not know is extremely stressful. The location of my delivery, whether from the pulpit or while walking around, depends on the leading of the Spirit and is related mainly to the type of message or else the style of worship. The style of delivery is not very important; I want to preach the word as I feel led by God's Spirit, and I continue to enjoy best the feeling that I am being used by God to bless somebody with the word of God.

Making the Right Choice*
Joshua 24:14-15, 21-28

Some years ago when we moved to the United States, we lived in Evanston, Illinois. I was attending the seminary. It took me time to adjust my life to the American culture, but I made many friends who were very helpful to me to get acquainted with American life and understand different perspectives of life. However, one of the things that took a long time to adjust to or to get used to was how to order food from a menu at a restaurant. My wife, Berth, and I were expecting our first child, John. I am sure most mothers will agree that during the time of pregnancy not all foods are delicious, but my wife became a good friend to the Chinese restaurants.

We went to different Chinese restaurants where they served buffets, and personally I did not have any problem because I could see what the food looked like and the choice was easy to make. One day we decided to go to a Chinese restaurant where we had to choose what we wanted to eat from a menu. To me, that was a nightmare. I can't remember the name of the food I chose, but my wife made her choice after she asked for help from a waitress. Brothers and sisters, I was hungry, but by the time the food was served on the table, my food was not as enjoyable as expected. However, my wife's choice was really tasty. We had to help each other and finally ended up by sharing my wife's plate because she had made the right choice.

Our message today is about making the right choice. Our Old Testament reading this morning reminds us of the account of Joshua with the children of Israel and their long trip in the wilderness. They did make it to the promised land, the land that God promised their ancestor Abraham, the land that flowed with milk and honey. This text also reminds us of the last days of Moses' leadership, as he knew that his days in this world were coming to an end.

After the death of Moses, Joshua took over the leadership of the people of Israel to lead them into the promised land. It is true this journey was not an easy one; it was a long journey with several challenges. Many of the challenges the people of Israel experienced

* This sermon was preached at Nashua UMC on February 27, 2011, the eighth Sunday after Epiphany. View the preaching of this sermon on www.garrett.edu/styberg-bump/lundula

14

in the wilderness were caused by their unfaithfulness to their God, the God of their ancestors Abraham, Isaac, and Jacob. On several occasions, the people turned away from God and were forced to repent from their wrongdoing. The question I try to ask myself about the unfaithfulness of these people to God was, why did it happen that way? It might be possible that many of these people were born in the wilderness. I am sure some of them did not experience the wonders that the group Moses led out of Egypt saw on the night they left Egypt. I am sure they heard the story, but they did not see the mighty hand of God, and so it was easy for them not to remain faithful to God whenever they were facing challenges.

Joshua was an important person who deserved to lead the children of Israel because he was somebody who knew the history of that long journey from Egypt to the promised land. He was someone who saw and experienced the mighty hand of the Lord when God divided the Red Sea and also the Jordan River to allow them to continue their journey. He was someone who remained faithful to the covenant they made with God, regardless of the challenges they went through in the wilderness. He was also someone who worked closely with Moses and led the people of God to the promised land after the death of Moses. Joshua was one of the two persons (Joshua and Caleb) from among the people who left Egypt with Moses who made it into the promised land.

Knowing that he did not have much time with them, Joshua prepared the people to make the right choice to continue serving their God faithfully. According to the Bible, Joshua gathered all the tribes of Israel (he did not forget any). He called all the elders, all the heads of families, and all the judges of Israel to a place known as Shechem to challenge them to make the right choice. Shechem was already an important place in the history of Israel. Shechem was the place where Abraham built the first altar to make a sacrifice to the Lord after he was called by God to leave his family and nation to go to the place which God prepared for him. And later, after the conquest of Canaan, Shechem became an important religious center in Israel, as it was also considered the city of refuge. Shechem was the place where Joseph's bones were buried after they moved to the promised land. It was the place where Joshua called the assembly of Israel to remember their covenant with God, to make the right choice to serve the God who gave them the promised land.

Why did he do all this? I am sure Joshua knew these people very well; he knew their strengths and also their weaknesses. He knew how easy it was for them to be drawn away from God to the worship of other gods that they found in the land where they were; how easy it would be to be seduced by that moment of victory and hope, after they had defeated the people who lived in the land and overthrown their gods. Joshua challenged the people of God to choose whom they would serve, but Joshua did not only present the different choices to them; he also helped them by showing them the right choice, the choice he made for himself and his household. He said to them, "Now if you are unwilling to serve the LORD, choose this day whom you will serve, whether the gods your ancestors served in the region beyond the River or the gods of the Amorites in whose land you are living; but as for me and my household, we will serve the LORD" (Joshua 24:15).

By saying "me and my household" Joshua referred to the people who lived with him. These could be his military people and servants, as well as his relatives. According to Joshua, the condition for these people to continue enjoying the blessing of the land God gave them and the victory God gave them over other nations was based on the decision they had to make on that day, the decision to choose to serve and worship God, and to keep their covenant with God, who saved them from the oppression of the Egyptians.

Brothers and sisters, as it was with the children of Israel and their journey in the wilderness, to experience different challenges until they got to their destination where they experienced victory over other people and their gods at God's hand, our every day in this world is a journey. Each day is a journey through which we are also called to overcome the different challenges of our time; a journey through which we are called to overcome the "gods of this land" until we get to our final destination that God promised us, the promise of God's kingdom through Jesus Christ. Our inheritance of this promise is based on the choice that we make today to accept Christ as our personal Lord and Savior.

As we go through our days in this world, as we enjoy the blessing of each other, the many blessings God has given us through our families, our church, our community, our nation, as it was with the children of Israel, we too have to know that we are also surrounded by many other "gods" of our time. These "gods" can be anybody or anything that can challenge our choice to remain faithful to God and also our choice to continue serving our God. These "gods" can be anything that interferes with the right choice we have made to follow Jesus Christ.

In the Gospel according to Matthew 6:24, Jesus said, "No one can serve two masters; for a slave will either hate the one and love the other, or be devoted to the one and despise the other. You cannot serve God and wealth." By talking about wealth in this passage, Jesus does not call us to renounce wealth; we need wealth for our survival, for our physical well-being, and even to support the work of the gospel of Christ. But Christ wants us to understand that the decision to choose and serve God is still the best and the right choice, and we should allow nothing to compete with that choice, including wealth. It is a call to choose to love, to honor, and to serve God with the same kind of devotion with which a slave would serve his or her master.

My friends, we know that we are also surrounded by foreign gods in the same way that the Israelites were surrounded by the gods of the Canaanites and Amorites, and they can affect our choice to follow and to serve God. Also, as we look around, we can agree that there are still many people in our communities, in our towns, in our families, in our nation, and also in our world who are struggling to make the right choice to accept and follow Christ. That is why today's world needs people like Joshua who can challenge the church to make the right choice to serve Jesus Christ. Today's church needs people like Joshua who can stand with courage and consider the future of the church by helping our children, our neighbors, our community, and our household to make the right decision to serve Christ and to believe in him as our personal Lord and Savior. Today's church needs people like Joshua who can stand and help the people of God to make the right choice to remain faithful to God and also to live the teachings of our Lord and Savior Jesus Christ.

Sometimes, depending on what we are experiencing in our daily life, in our families, in our churches, and also in our communities, it might be difficult to make the right choice that enables us to remain faithful to God. Brothers and sisters, regardless of our weaknesses, our challenges, our confusion, the different gods that surround us, the good news is that as we journey together in this world, we are not alone. We also have people to help us make the right decision. That day in the restaurant the waitress helped my wife to make the right choice, and in our lives we have the Holy Spirit to help us. The Holy Spirit journeys with us, empowers us, encourages us in our weakness, and helps us overcome the challenges presented by the gods of this time, so that we can make the right choice to serve Christ Jesus, to accept him as our personal Lord and Savior.

Brothers and sisters, this is a day of decision making, a day to make the right choice. For those who have already made that choice, let me conclude this message by calling your attention to think of that day, the day you accepted Christ Jesus as your personal Lord and Savior, the day you made your choice to become a member of this congregation; and today are you still living according to that choice? If you haven't made that choice, this is a day of a new beginning, a day of renewal, a day of decision making, a day to accept and serve Christ Jesus as your personal Lord and Savior.

I invite each one of you to a brief moment of silence as we reflect on that happy day, the day that we made our choice to follow Christ Jesus, the day of our new beginning. And for those who haven't made that choice, let this moment of reflection be an opportunity to make the right choice to accept Jesus Christ as your personal Lord and Savior. Now is the time, make the right choice.

CHAPTER THREE

To the Measure of Christ

Gregory Palmer

The goal of preaching is to help Christians, individually and in the community, to know God as seen in the life of Israel and made known intimately in Jesus Christ. Scripture provides us with word pictures of the people and events that give witness to the presence of God in the lives of God's people. As preacher of the word of God, my hope is to connect the hearers with the biblical stories in a way that will help them recognize the presence of God in their own lives and share the good news that God is with us in every time and place.

There is good news for all time and for every moment. God's self-giving in Jesus Christ comes to us where we are, and the good news of the sermon is the word that sets the hearer free to live the life God in Christ Jesus intends for them. In every moment of preaching, my intention is to help equip the people of God to confront the life and death issues that we face in our daily encounters. The setting and context in which the sermon is delivered are the key drivers that determine the direction in which the sermon will go. It is important that the hearers of the sermon see themselves in the message in the same way that they are led to see the people in the biblical stories that are the foundation of the sermon.

In order to bring this to pass, I put a lot of energy into understanding the context of the sermon at many levels, from the macro to the micro. The situations of the culture and of society—both nationally and worldwide—are important to the development of the message. Even when I am not actively preparing a sermon, I am constantly thinking about preaching and sermons because I am listening always for a message that God would like me to bring to the people of God. The process is ongoing for me; however, for a particular sermon I try to let myself marinate in the text through reading it and literally hearing it. I then proceed to try to articulate in my words a key message conveyed by the text. I do not assume there is only one key message that can be conveyed. But I try to focus on one.

The challenge of selecting a text is also a process of discernment. In the main, I prefer working with the lectionary text because I believe its use lends itself to developing the whole body of Christ, and it stretches my task as preacher and keeps me from preaching in my comfort zone only. However, I am often led to one particular scripture passage among the four texts provided that seems to offer the message God wants me to deliver; or I may be inspired to preach a message that seems to arise from one or more of the texts. The style and structure of the sermon arises from the content of the message and, since I am comfortable in both genres, may be topical or expository. The message is what is important; it is the mission of every preacher.

Our mission is nothing less than "New Creation." We are called to help the people of God see the new thing that God is doing in our midst. God calls us to offer a message of life, of hope, of peace and justice. There will be no world made new without peace and justice and, I would add, love—the love of God for all people. My hope is that through my preaching the hearers will experience God's presence in a way that says to each person: "You are a beloved child of God, and you can live like it." Working to get this message across energizes my preaching, stimulates my delivery, and guides the message whether it is delivered from the pulpit or in the midst of the congregation. As I develop the material that I take into the pulpit, I am guided by what I believe God would have me say.

My development as a preacher has been influenced deeply by my father, the Reverend Herbert E. Palmer, a preacher of the gospel whose years of preaching taught me the importance of delivering God's message faithfully to the people of God. The soul-stirring preaching of the Reverend Frank L. Williams also helped me understand the importance of reaching the people at their point of need. I understood from the responses of the people to these pulpit giants and even from my own preaching that people do indeed give an ear to the message. The people are listening to the voice of the preacher, but they are really listening for a word from God.

The challenge for me as a preacher, and in fact for each and every preacher, as a messenger of God's love, is to know how best in our frantic age to invite the full engagement of the hearer. The word of God is received first in the ear, but the hearer must allow that word to touch the mind and penetrate the heart in order for the message of God's love to give light to their life. As Christians individually and in the gathered community as the church, the body of Christ, our hope is to know God and see God's presence as revealed in scripture and in the world. Christians, the evidence of God's love is made known fully and intimately in Jesus Christ. It is Christ revealed in us, revealed in the words of the sermon, revealed in the moment of preaching that offers a message of hope to the hearers of the sermon. In the moment of preaching, the preacher becomes the voice of God to the hearers, calling them to accept the fullness of Christ for the living of their lives. My ultimate aim in preaching is to assist the hearers, individuals and their communities, to grow to the full measure of the stature of Jesus Christ.

Trustworthy Prophets[*]
1 Samuel 3:1-10

I want to talk to you tonight about being trustworthy prophets. It is easy to pick up the newspaper on any given day or to go to your favorite channel of receiving news, whether it's through the internet, on cable television, or network television, and walk away with the conclusion that we live in a world with an enormous trust deficit. And whether or not the trust deficit has to do with Wall Street or with BP oil or with large institutional churches, everybody in here tonight knows that we live in a world with an enormous trust deficit. People are cynical; they are suspicious of each other; they don't choose to trust each other; they believe they have valid reasons not to trust each other. But it's not really anything new.

If you are a serious student of history, you know that in most epochs of history there have always been these profound seasons in which the mistrust or the trust deficit was more acute or more heightened than in other times. We happen to be living in one of those acute times. I know that because I read the Bible. And when I read 1 Samuel 3 and the first couple of verses where the historian announces that the word of the Lord was rare in those days and visions were not widespread, I look back to chapter 2 and I flip back to chapter 1 and I wonder how did Israel get to this point that the historian would note that the word of the Lord was rare and that visions were not widespread?

Looking back, one gets the sense that something was wrong with temple life and the life of the current resident priestly family. The priests had lost their grip on what it was they were supposed to be doing; an enormous trust deficit developed. The people were not being nurtured and fed as they needed to be; the nation was without spiritual direction. You see, when the institution is faithful and strong in its witness and proclamation and ritual life, it has an anchoring effect on the lives of communities and nations. But the temple at Shiloh had gotten off track, and the priesthood had become

[*] This sermon was preached at the 2010 Ordination service of the Illinois Great Rivers Annual Conference. View the preaching of this sermon on www.garrett.edu/styberg-bump/palmer

corrupt because it had become all about them. I stopped by tonight to tell you ordinands, this is your night, but it isn't all about you. I love you tonight, preachers, but it isn't all about you. God knows it's not about me. In fact the thing that was so corrupt was that the sons of Eli were using their priestly role for self-aggrandizement. That's all that needs to be said really, when it becomes all about you. It isn't about our God, it isn't about the Christ of God, it isn't about the mission, it isn't about the transformation of the world—it's about how can I take care of me.

I want you to know tonight that all of you look pretty well-fed. God knows I do. Maybe we don't need to be taken care of, and God knows we don't have to grasp and to grab in such ways that there is no mission worth pursuing other than flagellating and satisfying our own needs. Now my baptized friends who do not happen to be licensed, consecrated, or ordained, I do not want you to be at ease in Zion tonight; because what can happen to us in these roles happens in local congregations and in annual conferences and in denominations because it becomes all about us. Let me give you a little "all about us" litany: "we never did it that way before; we don't want that kind of people in here." It can happen to us as individuals in our personal discipleship and in the practice of our ministry, and it can happen to the institutional representation of the gospel in the world until somebody announces that the thing has gotten so bad that the trust deficit is not just people to people.

The historian announced that he was saying that even God had lost faith in the current administration at Shiloh when he said: "The word of the LORD was rare." Meaning nothing I hear coming out of that temple is worth my time or attention. That is a sorry state, when it can be said by anyone that what we are doing in the church is not worth their time or attention. And there are so many ways in which this thing has become subtly corrupted not because we are inherently bad, but just because we have lost the edge and it's become a little bit about taking care of us—and that would be all of us—so that our voices are muted. And our mission is unclear. And why should anybody pay attention to anything that we have to say if they cannot see the profound alignment between our words and our practice?

So looming over this text is this tragic announcement. The word of the Lord was rare in those days, and visions were not widespread.

Welcome to ministry in the twenty-first century. So what are we going to do about it? And as I've already said to this class of ordinands, my yearning for you is that you would join us in being trustworthy prophets and where there is a trust deficit be so clear about who and whose we are and what it is that we are doing that at the end of the day, when the record is read (the old folks would say when the roll is called up yonder), when the roll is called up yonder, somebody—and I am mostly concerned about God— would say there were trustworthy prophets in Illinois Great Rivers. I maybe couldn't find them anywhere else, but in Central and Northern Illinois near the great rivers, I found a few trustworthy prophets; a few. And I think the way we get to be trustworthy prophets and a trustworthy church is by learning the practice and the discipline and the patience of discerning, listening again.

Because this is fundamentally a call story, part of what the historian is saying is that even when there is an enormous gap in trust, and even when God is a part of those who have become mistrustful or lacking in confidence about what is going on, God does not give up on God's mission. It's clear. The mission remains the same. The mission is to seek and pursue relentlessly nothing else but new creation. Everywhere there is death, our word is resurrection. Everywhere there is despair, our word is hope. Everywhere there is darkness, our witness is light. God goes to the temple and says, Samuel, Samuel! And he goes scurrying to Eli. He has no clue as to what is going on. Eli said, "I didn't call you, go back to sleep, let me go back to sleep," and the cycle repeats a couple of times. But Samuel is listening. He does not recognize the voice; he only recognizes his name; and he only believes the person summoning him is the adult party in whose charge he has been left—but he is attentive. So what would it look like for us to be attentive in an intense way, even if the first time we mistook the direction?

Because we are so messed up sometimes (not all the time), we are so paralyzed by fear we won't scurry in any direction, and if we are going to get out of this malaise we are going to have to take some risks, perhaps even the risks of misunderstanding and of being misunderstood. But I came by to tell you tonight that I refuse to sit here until I die. I refuse. And I want you to refuse, and I want all of you in your local churches to say, "I refuse to be a church where the Spirit of God has left the temple." Now, I didn't say you could go from five to five thousand folks, but you can live with such faithfulness and devotion that every time someone comes across you or comes across the path of somebody from your church, they will know that something is going on. So do something. Take some risks. You might fail, you might be wrong, you might misunderstand that the direction was here and you only moved this far, but by God's grace and God's abounding mercy you can engage in a course correction until you get on the path. But don't hear the voice, feel the nudge, and do nothing. God will hold you accountable for not responding at all. God can work with you even if you mistook the direction. I've been worked with, I know.

So after three times, Eli, half asleep, perhaps awakened so many times now that he couldn't go back to sleep, perceived that it just might be that the Lord was speaking to the lad. Now we who are eavesdropping on this call narrative understand that it has already been noted by the historian that Samuel did not yet know the Lord, had not come to spiritual maturity. His senses of discernment were not acutely developed. And Eli is an old blind man, spiritually numb in some way, grieving the loss of how he had let this thing slip away from him. I don't know everything I need to know, and we all need mentors. And even that which you think is useless isn't completely out of business until God says so. And God was relentless in the purpose, said I've got to get me a new trustworthy, listening, obedient, servant prophet. And he is alone tonight in the temple with an old blind man, and sure enough didn't the spirit of God lead Eli. As if to say, "Old man, I need you for one last engagement."

So even though you know you got it all together, don't cast the rest of us old heads aside. Lay, clergy: don't throw us to the side, don't throw us under the bus, because you're going to face something and you're not going to have a clue, even if you know what's happening, how to get out of it—not because you're not smart but just because you have not seen that movie before. And we may not be much, but we've seen the movie before and we know how it ends. Am I right? Am I right? Am I right? So if God is willing to use us, let God use us until God uses us up. Because it is with that partnership of the new and old among all of the baptized that God is going to get God's program back on track. So, trustworthy prophets, learn to listen! And then learn the skills of really listening!

25

Eli, even in his somewhat infirm state, said, "Son, go back, lie down in your place, and if you hear that same voice again, simply say, 'Speak, Lord, your servant is listening.'" An old washed-out priest played his part in keeping God's program going at Shiloh. And sure enough, Samuel did it. He didn't know anything else to do. So naive as not to understand the dangers of saying, "Speak, for thy servant is listening." Because you know there is a certain comfort in being truly ignorant. So Samuel said, "Speak, your servant is listening." I am here to tell you, if you really don't want to know about God's future for you, please don't ask, because God just might take you seriously. And it will rearrange your life. If you say, "Speak, Lord, your servant is listening," buckle up your seatbelts, put on your crash helmet, get your flares because you're about to be messed up. I know I am right; it's right there in the Bible. And God said to Samuel what I am about to do is going to make you and all of Israel's ears tingle, because I am about to bring one priestly line to a close and I am about to install new leadership, because I am relentless in the pursuit of my purpose.

And in a moment Samuel had flash before him the complete changing of his life, the complete subversion of the way things were to the way things might become. Oh my God, if you don't want to know then don't ask it, because it will give you more than indigestion. It will demand everything of you. Samuel was so frightened by what he heard from the Lord God that he was disquieted the rest of the night. But early in the morning Eli wanted to know what was going on. What did our God say? What did the creator of the universe say? What did the one who brought us out of bondage in Egypt say? What did the one who gave the commandment on the holy mountain say? And Samuel was utterly afraid, about to crawl up in the fetal position. And then Eli starts threatening him, "If you don't tell me, may God do to you even worse than whatever God disclosed to you about us." And so with fear and trembling, Samuel told him. Eli said, "Come on, I can take it." In fact it's already been disclosed to me, I just need you to confirm. So here is the last step in being a trustworthy prophet: tell the truth. I know it's hard to tell the truth to folks that write your paycheck. But in the long scheme of things, if we don't tell the truth and they hear the truth somewhere else, they will despise us. Tell the truth. Preach the word, in season, out of season.

We've got a world to save and a God to glorify. Tell the truth. What I say to you I say to all of you. Not just those who got these funny-looking things around their shoulders but to all of you. Now we can all do some growing, but let me get real with you here. We are not perishing really for a lack of knowledge. We just don't want access to the knowledge we already have because it demands conversion. Why should I get converted? I mean, things have been going on all right. And we need to be converted because God is in relentless pursuit of the mission and has graciously invited us to join God in bringing new creation. I don't know if you think about legacy in the sense of what will people say when you're done—done at a particular appointment, done with decades of ministry. But I tell you old Samuel got one heaven of a postscript. God let not one of his words fall to the ground. And from then to Beersheba, geographically, he will be known as a trustworthy prophet. I want to be a trustworthy prophet. I want all of us to preach and teach and baptize and serve to be trustworthy prophets. And I want to be supported and nurtured by a trustworthy church. And I am begging you tonight, for the sake of the reign of God, let's get with the program.

In the name of the Father, and of the Son, and of the Holy Ghost. Let all of God's people say: Amen.

CHAPTER FOUR

The Liberating Word of God

Vance P. Ross

I view the power of preaching as the divine and contemporary word of God, releasing humans from any imprisoning or enslaving element. This view reflects a theology of preaching as liberating and is built primarily from Isaac Rufus Clark's definition of preaching. Clark defines preaching as "substantially divine activity, wherein the Word of God is proclaimed or announced on contemporary issues, with a view towards ultimate response to our God."[1] Preaching is God-breathed declaration, confronting issues of the day with the expectation that hearers must respond. That response is related directly to the transformation that the hearers experience, which results from the liberating word of God offered by the preacher.

That word comes to the hearers in different ways but finds relevance in its appropriateness to their lives for the particular time and place. To say that sermonic discourse is timeless means that it was good for its time and has been found relevant in eras since it was first preached. Preaching that fails to speak to its era and age is, in my view, not preaching, and the preacher is charged with the responsibility of helping people experience the freeing grace of God for the living of their lives in the present. Sermons must point to victorious perseverance. In the words of a Johnny Ray Youngblood sermon, we are "the overcoming crowd," which means that through the good news of Jesus Christ the hearers can overcome sin and the challenges of life. The assurance of this good news is present in scripture and provides the basis for preaching.

Whether preaching as appointed pastor or as guest preacher, I look consistently to "exegete the people." Context is everything. By context I mean what happens in neighborhood, community, city, county, state, and nation. In order to prepare to preach, I begin by looking at the people. What is happening in this time, in this place, and in this era? Is the ecclesial calendar offering a topic or need that must be addressed? Does the lectionary speak to this moment? The preacher must address, through the biblical text, some or all of these questions in order to be relevant and beneficial to God's people. For my preaching, this is absolutely essential, and explicitly or implicitly, I hope to assist hearers to see the relevance of the biblical context as I preach. In this way the sermon reflects my understanding, as preacher, of the context of the hearers' lives.

Contemplating the environment and situation(s) of the hearers fundamentally impacts the choice of scripture texts for preaching. The Revised Common Lectionary assists often as a source for finding texts for preaching; however, even with that, choices are determined based on the situation of those who are to hear the sermon. I believe that all preaching needs to be expository; the biblical text must confront topics, "exposing" the issues to divine truth. To offer clarification of scripture without it speaking to a particular situation in life for a particular people is, from my point of view, of little value. Expository preaching is my preference, but, having said that, I believe topical discourse is vitally important. However, it is best confronted by exposing God's response to the situation through biblical texts. That response is made to a particular people in a particular context. I use other available resources such as Nave's Topical Bible or other internet resources to help find a text for preaching, and with the context in mind, I try diligently to get a sense of how the text feels or speaks to me.

Every sermon requires that the preacher engage a process of study and interpretation, and I use various types of biblical tools in order to develop what Dr. Clark called "the Anatomy of the Idea."[2] The nucleus or foundation of that idea is based on the good news of salvation. The sermon provides the opportunity for sharing God's living Word, Jesus Christ—what he said and did, through God's written Word—so that people can hear and receive the message of God's saving love. The message that the sermon offers, the message of God's love, invites the hearers into kingdom living that offers peace and justice. It is the message of Jesus of Nazareth, the one we also call the Christ, who was born and lived in a context of political and economic injustice. He taught and demonstrated— spiritually, politically, and socially—that divinity confronts, protests against, and loves people such that these injustices can change. In this way preaching becomes both pastoral and prophetic. In fact I believe preaching is pastoral because it is prophetic (truth-telling), and therefore issues of justice and peace are essential to the content of my sermons.

Over the many years of preaching, my process of sermon development, my style of sermon, and my delivery of the message have all developed and changed in many ways. I created manuscripts for twenty-three years, and then for the past three and a half years I have been unable to write full manuscripts. I do not understand why; however, I do find that it has me interacting more with the congregation. Over this same time, I find that I do walk around much more, and I have come to define my delivery style as intelligent enthusiasm. But whatever the style may be, my hope in preaching is that people will hear God's word and that my sermonic discourse moves people to become better citizens in the Commonwealth of God. I hate "flunking" before the people; even more, I hate flunking before God.

Notes

1. This quotation is from notes taken in a class taught by Isaac Rufus Clark, Preparation and Delivery of Sermons, in the 1983–84 school year at Gammon/Interdenominational Theological Center.
2. Ibid.

Beyond the Cave Crisis[*]
1 Kings 19:11-18

It is basketball season, 1962, Bluefield, West Virginia. That itty-bitty, teenie-tiny town is nestled in the southwesternmost corner of West Virginia, up high, so high that it is called "nature's air conditioned city." It was basketball season at Park Central High School in 1962. I could only have been five years old, approaching my sixth year, when Hershel A. Ross, my late father, came to see my mother. There must have been some sort of romantic nocturnal interlude, because in July of 1963, Vince Darryl Ross was born: baby brother. There were already Donnie and Ronnie, and Lady, who was between them. I thought a gift had come especially for me. There was Vance and Vince. I thought that I had given him the name myself, but my mother told me later that I came single, Donnie and Ronnie came double, and her plan was to have twin boys that were to be named Vance and Vince; and since it took so long, my baby brother is Vince.

Vince, my baby brother, left with my mother's aunt to go to New York, because we were a family on public assistance. We called it welfare in those days, and there was so many of us—five of us. There was some sense that the government might cut off some assistance because of what they would call "irresponsible behavior." My brother went to New York with my aunt and grew up on the street of Bedford-Stuyvesant in Brooklyn, New York. He graduated from Westinghouse High School. You wouldn't know a lot about Westinghouse except that Jayzee, who was born five minutes away from there, went to school there. My brother and others who came out of that school talked about it as if it were Fort Apache, but not in the Bronx. This was a place where you went to learn how to be a criminal, but somehow my baby brother escaped and came back to West Virginia to go to college and graduated from West Virginia State College. While he was there, finances for school began to dwindle, and he needed to find a way to be in school and so he joined the ROTC. He did not intend to be in there long, just long enough to pay that school bill, but he got in there and began

[*] This sermon was preached at the 2011 Convocation for Pastors of Black Churches held in Nashville, Tennessee. View the preaching of this sermon on www.garrett.edu/styberg-bump/ross

to like the money, and he liked moving around a bit. So my brother became a distinguished graduate of ROTC. Vince went on to the army and got a command as a Second Lieutenant. He was so good as a Second Lieutenant and he was such a good leader that they decided to fast-track him to Fort Benning, Georgia, and he finds himself in an airplane with some other brothers. He felt good getting in the airplane, and everybody had to jump out of the plane with a parachute in order to go forward to become a Captain. Then he remembers he does not like heights. Not only does he not like heights, he does not have any sort of sense that he ever wants to act like or behave like he wants to jump out of something. He does not want to ride a roller coaster, and now he is on an airplane, and he is there waiting to jump out of an airplane. I can't tell you everything he is saying, but you can imagine what he is saying: "I didn't want to be a part of the Army. I just did this to pay for school. I did not realize that when they said to me I was going to move along, that meant I was going to have a parachute on my back. Why am I up here with these fools? How in the world did I get here?"

That is where Elijah is. Elijah has been doing his thing a chapter or two before. You recall he has a duel on the mountain with all the bad boys of Baal, and he calls the fellows out. He says, "Look a here, y'all so bad, let's see if we can get something burning up here and see who really is bad." They tried. They prayed and hollered and were screaming. Can't you see him? Yeah! Yeah! Ain't nothing happening. Where is your god? Is there a "your" god? Can't get nothing done. They start cutting themselves, then they said look a here. Then Elijah says, "Look a here, let me show you how bad my God is. Go get some water, get a whole lot of water. Get as much water as your water people can bring. Bring your water, people. Bring that water, 'cause we getting ready to deal with this thing. I won the battle, but now I am going to win the war." For the non-militaristic United Methodist Black preachers in the room, I am not attempting here to justify what happens militarily or violence. I am just reporting.

This cat takes everybody out. He tells Ahab, "Look here, brother, get some stuff straight. I am trying to tell you who the real God is." And Ahab runs to his woman, Jezebel. Imagine with me, if you would. I can imagine it this way: Jezebel, or Sis, says, "You disloyal, no good, milquetoast weakling! You tell that boy Elijah that me and you are going to get him, and get him good." Our boy, Elijah, who just beat the bad boys of Baal, is now on the run based on what Jezebel and Ahab have laid out. He is scared to death. He says, "How did I get here?"

Let me get a little closer here. Church officers are saying we've got to move. How did I get here? I just said to you all that your methods are not only non-Christian but often ungodly. How did I get here?

Appointment in trouble; apportionments ain't paid; this church doesn't look like it is growing the way we want to see it grow. It doesn't matter how many people you're claiming are in here if the money ain't coming. How did I get here?

It occurs to me that sometime some folk miss the fact that disciples of Jesus are not created in a day. That isn't just for cabinets and bishops, though; this is for some lay folk and preachers. Nobody became disciples of Jesus because you whooped. Nobody became disciples of Jesus because you read the *Discipline* through, nobody became a disciple of Jesus because you have the best praise team since Carter made liver pills. But now, because it is taking time and teaching, I am moving? How did I get here?

Can I get closer, still? Why are my colleagues mad with me? I can't make the Jurisdictional Conference elect me in 1996 and 2000? Why are my colleagues mad with me? I can't make somebody appoint me? All I did was preach the best I could. All I did was teach the best I could. All I did was be faithful to where I was. How did I get here?

My dear United Methodist Black pastors and church leaders, brothers and sisters, I choose now to define myself as a United Methodist Black man, not a Black United Methodist man. Here is why: I was born male. I was born Black. Even though the only church I ever went to was United Methodist, my United Methodism is a choice. My maleness and Blackness are gifts from God. Therefore, I define myself as that which at the end is closer to God. Man, Black man, United Methodist Black man. I believe we ought to be proud of our heritage, proud of our culture, proud of our people—and so should my less than Black sisters and brothers. My understanding is that all people come from a Black woman in Africa. If that's true, then all people are Black people. Some are just not as Black as others. So my less than, my not so Black sisters and brothers need to love themselves, love their culture, and we all love it all together. God did not make a mistake. God did not make no junk. So I am not going to act like something is optional when it is in fact foundational. I believe that God gifted me to be a Black man, and God gifted us with Black church and Black culture. Yet so often our denominational options of affiliation trump our God-gifted and God-created obligations.

Dear sisters and brothers, how did we get here? We got here because we stopped listening to God. We started listening to Jezebel and Ahab. You know the member with big money and little Jesus. Jezebel and Ahab, the so-called leaders, the so-called big person, and when you check it out, they just giving a little bit of money and no Jesus, just got a big mouth. We start listening to anybody, anywhere, anytime, except the one that empowered us to deal with the bad boys to start with. Except the one who called us, invited us, and dared us to be in this gospel ministry. Except the one who put a stamp on us and gave us, as Jeremiah A. Wright said, "a designer label meant to beat all designer labels, made in the image of God." We are in the cave crisis because we listened to someone else. But the cave ain't the problem, because we are hearing the voice anyway. The cave ain't our issue. Our issue is the fear that results from listening to our peculiar, particular, specific, contextual, environmental Ahabs and Jezebels, and it is in listening to these Ahabs and Jezebels that we get thrown out of our prophetic gift and role. Renita Thomas reminds us that the prophetic role is not about fortune-telling. It is about truth-telling. The prophetic role is not about being able to say I see money, money, money, money. The prophetic role is about telling God's truth in the context in which we find ourselves and trusting God to work it out as it is declared. And so we can get beyond this cave crisis if we pay attention to the whole of Elijah's work in ministry up to this point and recall it for ourselves.

To be prophetic is to be powerful. To be prophetic is to be pastoral. To be prophetic is to be connectional.

To be prophetic is to be powerful. This cat, in front of the king, by himself, went up on the mountain and whipped everybody. He did the Muhammad Ali, way ahead of the game. He had the original Spike Lee joint (to quote the title of one of Lee's finest films), he "did the right thing" and he did it out of the unction, the spirit of God, the Holy Spirit. He was able to be the conduit of power because the power was not in fortune-telling, it was in truth-telling. We've got to understand that to be prophetic is powerful because it is the truth.

Winston Churchill said, "Truth is incontrovertible; malice may attack, ignorance may defame it, but in the end, there it is." Truth cannot be destroyed. Truth cannot be devastated. Truth cannot be overwhelmed. Truth cannot be overcome. If we dare to stand and tell God's truth, when we dare to stand and speak God's truth, when we dare to preach the truth of God we may get whipped in the moment, but in the end we are going to be vindicated. God's truth cannot be shut off, can't be shut down, cannot be put away. God's truth is power. Brothers and sisters, we can get past this crisis. We can get past the cave crisis, but we must tell the truth.

It is vitally important that the Black preacher and the pastor of the Black church remember what it has meant for the Black church to be present in this denomination and in this nation and in this world. It was the Black church that was the place that rose people up to end enslavement. It was the Black church that gathered people together so that we would be desegregated. It was the Black church that put people in school, gave us libraries, hospitals, leadership, students, study; and if it is going to continue, we must not—we cannot—forget. Our denomination—our people—need the power of this truth. When we are enticed, when we are seduced, when we succumb to a misunderstanding and misappropriation of who God called us to be, when we become dealers in so-called financial prosperity rather than preachers and dealers in the abundant life, which is holistic and has something to do with something that is other than a dollar, we have walked away from our historic role and call. God has called us to a power that transcends Main Street and Wall Street, transcends even Pennsylvania Avenue. The truth of God is the most powerful thing in the universe. Brothers and sisters, we can get beyond this cave crisis. There is restoration for us, liberation for our community. We must understand that to be prophetic is to be powerful.

It is not just powerful; it's pastoral. Yes I know there was a lot of mayhem and murder in this and a lot of blood, gore, and all of that. Get past that: the text is telling us something has got to be cleaned up. It's some death out here that has to be straightened up, and we

36

have to kill some stuff to do that. The truth declares that it must happen.

I have two grandchildren. The boy is ten and the girl is nine. The boy came to visit me this summer. He came with a list of things that he wants to do when he comes. I wrote the list down and tried to do what my boy wanted to do 'cause I like the boy. I like his mother. She is my daughter. I like her, but he is more fun than she is. I asked him, "Christopher, what do you want to do?" He said, "I want to go to Chuck E. Cheese." I said, "You want to go to Charles Edward Cheese." He said, "No, his name is Chuck E." I said, "I want to call him Charles." He said, "His name is Chuck E." So we went to Chuck E. Cheese. Christopher and I are playing this game that has two remote controls, and he beats me. Christopher turns to me and says, "Pop Pop! You suck." Then he got this face on him. You know that face of 1960. How many of you came up in the sixties? Do you remember saying something that you ought not to have said to momma? I got that face once, in 1965. I was talking to my momma, and I made this noise. She *thought* I said something to her I should not have said. I saw the blur of her hands flashing toward my face! All I felt were my cheeks throbbing. That pain was the face of the 1960s. Christopher has this sixties look on his face.

What was really going on is, "Pop Pop, you are clearly incapable of playing this game. Your lack of experience and your woeful inability is so inadequate that you are messing everything up. Pop Pop, this is pitiful, pathetic, and terrible, the way you are trying to do this very elementary, rudimentary game that I can find a three- or four-year-old to play better than you. You are coming somewhere near some kind of retardation, Pop Pop, that I don't understand." But he did not have time to say all of that. So he just said, "Pop Pop, you suck!"

Sometimes, as pastors, the pastoral thing to do is to tell people, with love: you suck! Somebody needs to say, "We've got a lot of members, but nobody knows that this church is here; it does not make any difference. You suck." Somebody needs to say, "We've got people in this choir who have been singing since the Mississippi was a creek and their voice wasn't but so good back then! Now when they are singing it's so bad they are singing people *out* of the church. Choir, you suck." Some of us, as preachers, are standing behind the sacred desk taking five minutes to say absolutely nothing. We spent no time in study. We spent no time in prayer, and it shows. Whoever it is, me or you, Vance, preacher: you suck.

At some point we have got to understand that it is not lacking in pastoral integrity to tell the truth. Truth-telling is in point of fact pastoral. At some point, if it's racist, if it's sexist, if it's homophobic, if it is elitist, if it is ageist, if you are shutting people out, cutting people out, putting people down and claim you are following Jesus, somebody somewhere ought to say somehow, you suck and you need to change. You are sucking the air out, you are sucking the life out, you are messing this thing up and, at some point, truth has to be told whether or not it is politically correct. Whether or not it is the right time and space and place. Whether or not somebody finds it disagreeable. We can come out, but at some point we have got to understand that to be prophetic is to be powerful and to be pastoral. If you can find a sweet, pretty, cute, satin, silk tongue, silver way to say the truth, please do. But when it is not getting through to Vance, when it is not being heard by Johnnie, when somehow, some place, in some space it is going over Cynthia's head, Christopher Bryant Harris, tell them like you told Pop Pop, "You suck!" We can get better. We ought to get better. We can get bigger because the almighty God so demands.

There aren't any more important people than empowered lay people. Don't get this twisted. This "ain't going to roll" just because of pastors. We have got to empower some lay folk. We've got to make some lay ministries and lay ministers who can make it happen and we can truly change the world in Jesus' name. Make disciples of Jesus, not just disciples. A whole lot of people have disciples. We ought to make disciples of Jesus. We can get beyond the cave crisis. We must remember that to be prophetic is to be powerful and to be pastoral.

We've got much to do. God will bless us to do it when we understand that being prophetic is powerful; it is connectional. When you look at the text, and Elijah is talking about everything bad happening, he acts like nothing bad has happened before. He is here all by himself and the voice of sheer silence reminds him, not only did you kill some people, you are getting ready to anoint some kings. You are getting ready to put some people in some spots in some places. They are going to clean some mess up, and you are going to find out that I have a guy who is waiting to be taught by you. He is going to be out there, and in addition there are seven thousand who did not bow down, who have not gotten on their knees, who are out there. You are not isolated. You are not by yourselves. You are not alone. You are connected. You are connected.

My baby brother, Vince Darryl, who is now a Lieutenant Colonel in the Army, who was scared to death of heights, did not want to be in that plane, did not want to jump out of that plane. He told me, "Vance, I got out of that plane because I looked up after I finished all that and saw somebody at the door. The somebody at the door is called a jump master. A jump master says to you, everything is clear. The jump master says to you, now is your time. The jump master says to you, we are ready for you and if it is right you are ready to go." Does anybody here need a jump master? Does anybody here know a jump master? I want to tell you the jump master is Jesus! Amen.

CHAPTER FIVE

Proclamation and Embodiment

Pamela Lightsey

I preached my first sermon when I was nineteen years old at Warner Street Church of God in Tacoma, Washington. The title was "Bearing That Bear!" and I remember the theme had to do with motivating and encouraging the listeners to keep their faith in God, persevering through the toughest of times. My pastor, the Reverend Faye Sandling, and the congregation of that tiny church were kind, and in Pentecostal form, "shouted" me up to a respectable conclusion. During those days, both my pastor and the Reverend Shirley Caesar, a fireball gospel singer known for her soul-stirring homilies imbedded within her songs, fed my soul and ended up being my early preaching "voice" and style. I understood any viable sermon as one that had "Holy Ghost fire" to the extent that the hearer felt compelled to salvific conversion, conviction, motivation, or sanctification.

These days, my theology of preaching leads me to view preaching as both proclamation and *embodiment*. Preaching is for me an embodiment of the love of God. *Proclamation* suggests a vocal enunciation, very often in a public setting. I have found—in this age of the bully pulpit and preachers who project a czar-type persona—that the most effective preaching actively demonstrates and embodies God's love throughout the preaching moment. People tend to "get" that even when the sermon misses the precise articulation of the good news. Good news, as I understand and preach it, is the love and providential care of God for all of creation in all times and in all seasons.

In fact, it is an attention to the good news of the gospel that is of primary importance to me as I translate into sermon format the "Word of God for the people of God" as they will come together in the preaching moment. That message is developed after hours of reading—scripture, newspapers, social network sites, blogs, classic books—and critical reflection. Most times, it is this rigorous studying that influences both the type of sermon—expository or topical—and the scripture text for preaching.

But how is this preaching developed? Am I an extemporaneous or manuscript preacher? I can say that I never enter the pulpit without having a prepared sermon. I believe I have a responsibility to offer those who come to hear me preach a most accurate account of the faith. For an extemporaneous sermon, I have an outline; for all others, I have a manuscript. I prefer manuscript simply because I am more comfortable pouring out on paper the gospel message and rehearsing it for inaccuracies in theology, logic, grammar, and paragraph transition. While I always critique myself rather harshly after most sermons, I find I am generally apt to use senseless fillers or offer unnecessary or inappropriate statements during extemporaneous sermons. Unless God directs, I avoid this style of preaching.

As for manuscript preaching, I never sit down to develop the sermon until I have "heard" myself preaching portions of it. This "hearing" comes after the text has been selected and I have read, re-read, and studied the text for several days. My goal is to know the text so well that if I somehow did not have access to the final manuscript (like the time it blew off the pulpit), I could still preach the sermon.

The lectionary helps me select an appropriate text. I prayerfully review the texts for the week considering what is happening in the world and within the community of the congregation. The text will be relevant to the context of the listener and to a particular theme that I feel impressed by the Holy Spirit to address (for instance, greed, depression, repentance). With theme and text in mind, I shape the most important part of the sermon: the thesis or topic. I keep this thought in mind: What lesson(s) do you want the listeners to learn as a result of this message? To answer this question I return to the text to let it show me the "points" for the sermon, the responses to the guiding question about what I want the listener to learn. This is where creativity comes into play. Taking those responses, I shape the body of the text as one would shape a short essay, dropping in illustrations where appropriate to keep the conversation lively, especially to keep the listeners engaged and not feeling as though I'm lecturing.

Because I am a social justice activist, I am not interested in developing sermons just for the sake of individuals feeling "good." I am interested in motivating persons to live in righteous communion with God. In this way, I am not too far removed from my earlier Pentecostal disposition. I really want the sermons I preach to influence the lives of the listeners. Therefore, I always preach with an ear for how my words are being delivered, with an intentional sensing for the energy in the room as well as trying to "feel" how I am connecting with the congregation. Multitasking? Not really. I like to think of it as "anointed preaching."

Finally—and this is the most challenging part about preaching for me—I must shape the conclusion. It must bring all points home. It must connect all the dots. It must leave the listeners thinking and give them pause to reconsider their own lives. Unlike at other points in the sermon, it is at the conclusion that I may step away from the pulpit, walking down to the front center aisle. The conclusion, if done correctly, can easily serve as the call to discipleship.

While it is not done at every event or every church I have the privilege of preaching for, the call to discipleship is my most rewarding experience of preaching. The manuscript has ended, but the preaching is still taking place. God is still using me, and I thoroughly enjoy standing before God's people, beckoning them to receive the good news of God's love and salvation in their lives— the perfect conclusion to the preaching moment.

If There Should Come a Word[*]
2 Kings 22:11-13; 23:1-3

Over fifty years ago, on February 1, 1960, four African American male students from North Carolina Agricultural and Technical College sat down on some stools at a lunch counter in a Woolworth's store in downtown Greensboro. And nothing happened—or so it seemed. The next day the four students came back and sat down again, and with them were twenty-seven other students, four of whom were women. And nothing happened! Word of what was taking place rapidly spread at NC Tech and in Greensboro, so much so that by February 5, three hundred students from across the city arrived at this tiny store. Things started getting tense, so on the sixth of February, members of the football team came along to serve as defense. But things were brought to an abrupt halt that day by a bomb threat. The owner now decided to shut the store down. And these peaceful yet prophetic sit-ins became the backbone of the Civil Rights Movement. But the sit-ins alone did not bring civil rights. That would require a bigger plan and many more participants. People who had a vision of a better world, the courage to get involved, and the faith to believe God would make it happen in their lifetime.

This morning, friends, we are gathered as the people of God, compelled by the gift of God called faith, to be challenged and inspired to be that authentic witness of God's love and justice to the world. In these times, where the faith of many is not processed, is not developing, but is as though it were in arrested development, the task of the believer is to remain committed to the faith so that, like the students at NC Tech, we receive the word that's spreading and have the courage to get involved for the betterment of the world.

It was this compelling, constructive faith in God which emboldened a young shepherd by the name of David to courageously stand up to Goliath and the Philistine army. It was faith that motivated David, right after he's anointed king of Israel and Judah, to do something bold and unique—to take two groups of people and

---

[*] This sermon was preached at Hemenway UMC in Evanston, Illinois, on Sunday, February 20, 2011. View the preaching of this sermon on www.garrett. edu/styberg-bump/lightsey

unite them as one. David believed that it could be done! This king, who held the throne many years before King Josiah, realized, unlike many of our national leaders today, that it takes more than the occupation of land and more than the establishment of a state capital to keep the two kingdoms of Israel and Judah together.

David realized that not even calling his countrymen together for the purpose of waging war to defeat a common enemy—the Philistines—that not even just war has the power to centralize and to unite a kingdom.

Military and political power alone is not enough to bring a quarreling and divided people together. But there is one source of strength, one source of hope, one source of joy in times of sorrow, one source of strength in times of weakness, one source of direction in times of blindness—and when the newly inaugurated King David recalls to his mind that sacred unifying object of loyalty among his people, he gathers (the Bible says) thirty thousand chosen men of Israel, and they set out to bring to Jerusalem that one sacred source that alone could unify a divided people. And so they mount up to get the Ark of the Covenant, that sacred emblem that declared the presence of God dwelling among them.

It is the Ark of God, you recall, that held within it the Decalogue—the Ten Commandments—and the Law of Moses. The Ark held the written covenant between God and God's people. It symbolized God's presence among them. It reminded the Israelites of God's wonder-working power for them. The Ark had traveled with them through the wilderness and came with them into the land of Canaan. This visible and tangible symbol that the God of their faith was with them was enough to make a grown man leap and dance and shout with all his might. It was enough to make David celebrate with unbelievable joy as he marched it into the city of Jerusalem.

Maybe you'll not be able to understand the faith of David if you've never experienced a season of spiritual emptiness. Maybe you'll not be able to understand the faith of David if you equate faith with perfection. Maybe you'll not be able to understand why David leaped and danced before the Ark if you've never endured the abuse of an oppressive leader, an oppressive supervisor, an abusive spouse or friend and God graciously and miraculously brought you through. Maybe you won't understand David's exuberance unless you've experienced faith, as Paul Tillich would describe it, as "the state of being grasped by an ultimate concern."[1] The state of being so in love, so captivated by Jehovah God, that your faith is to you, as the writer of Hebrews describes, as the eschatological "substance of things hoped for, the evidence [the conviction] of things not seen" (Hebrews 11:1 NKJV). Only through the tender eyes of faith willing to embrace the context of our scripture lesson can we understand why this new king, King Josiah, is so distraught.

The great kingdom, which David had brought together, is now divided. The people have given themselves over to disobedience and idolatry. King after king gave himself over to religious compromise and Yahweh, God of the people, who once held their absolute allegiance, has now become just another god among a pantheon of other deities. The Temple, which David's son Solomon built as the central place of worship for the united monarchy, has been plundered. The treasures and vessels dedicated to Yahweh have been looted. Idolatrous altars have been set up in the house of God, and spiritual decline prevails in the land. The people speak about God, but their hearts and actions are far removed from the loving faith of their great ancestors.

But then, right in the midst of this scene of spiritual death, the writer brushes onto the narrative canvas the details of the work of a new king in town! This king is not like the other kings before him; this king ushers in reform. This king commands the repair and renovation of the Temple; this king is compared to none other than David, for this king, Josiah, the text says *did what was right in the sight of the Lord.* King Josiah commanded the people to worship no other God but Yahweh. He tore down all the high places of idolatrous gods; he reestablished the keeping of the Passover; he instituted religious reform and ordered the cleanup and repair of the Temple.

Imagine this scene: As the Temple is being repaired, the high priest, whose duty it was to care for the Temple, is preparing the room where all the treasures are stored, and he sees a scroll tucked away among the treasures. And after he pulls it from among the treasures he unfolds it. Imagine him gasping as he reads the printed text. Realizing what it is, the high priest immediately sends word to the king that he has found the Book of the Law.

Let me lay this out for you again, friends, because I don't want you to miss this point: Here they are, working to repair the Temple of God, and they're standing in a room which they for many years understood as containing treasures, and yet there is one treasure tucked away in that room that, if taken to heart, has the potential of leading an entire nation to newness—not just a building to completion but a nation to total spiritual renovation. There it is, no longer hidden but in plain sight, the Book of the Law.

I want to remind you, my friends, this morning, that there is no treasure in this world, there are no riches on this planet, no sparkly, glittery, bling-blingy wealth on this earth that has more impact or more significance for our lives than the Word of God. You may tuck it away, you may cover it up, and you may ignore its presence. You may build for yourself houses and mansions on large expanses of land and place God's word on a corner table, let it collect dust or tuck it away on a shelf. But I assure you that God's word will not be hidden for long. God's word will not be forgotten for long. God will not allow that word to be tucked away forever, not even in the house of God!

But this text should lead us to some questions. You may ask me: Preacher, how can the word be hidden in the Temple of God? You may ask me: Preacher, how can the Book not be known to God's people who come to the Temple of God? You may ask me: Preacher, didn't they realize and know to do better than that? Well, look around. The world has often ignored the Word of God. For whenever you make the Word part of an earthly treasure that's when it's possible to have the Word in the Temple but not have the Word in your heart.

The slave masters had the Word in the church. They quoted the Word to the slaves, but they didn't have the Word in their hearts. During the era of Jim Crow, our legislators had the Word up on Capitol Hill, tucked away in the chambers of power, but they didn't have the Word in their hearts. The Mississippi police who beat down Fannie Lou Hamer had Bibles in their homes but not a Word in their hearts. The preachers who told Martin Luther King, Jr., to be patient and not to expect change overnight, told him not to be an agitator, they had the Word in their pulpits, but they didn't have it in their hearts.

We are here today, despite all the forces the perpetuators of injustice lined up to carry out their evil plots, because down through the ages God has always had someone, even when the Book sat amongst earthly treasures, who carried the *Word* in their heart.

And so it was that when King Josiah heard the words of the Book of the Law and tore his clothes, it was not because the book had been found but because he received the Word of God in his heart! The power of the Word is not the Book; it is the Spirit that illumines the Book. It will not be hidden. It will not be silenced. It will not be forgotten. It will not be idolized as a mere earthly treasure. When our hearts are right and we commit ourselves, like King Josiah, to do what is right and walk in the way of the Lord, God will send a word!

God still requires each and every one of us to serve God with the kind of religious vitality that demonstrates to the world that there is always more to our faith than what is written in the book. Always more to our faith than what is spoken from our lips. Always more to our faith than the quoting of scriptures. Always more to our faith than what is written in creeds or affirmations. Always more to our faith than what is preached. It's not what we read. It's not what we say. But it's what we live each and every day!

Over fifty years ago, four students sat at a lunch counter. They sat there having been raised up by a community of people who believed in our God who is just and righteous. They had no idea what would happen, but they trusted God and believed in the righteousness of their actions. And the word spread. And others joined. And God's justice prevailed. They lived their faith. They lived the Word. Where is the Word in your life? Does it sit on a shelf? Is it hidden among your treasures? I pray from this day forward the Word will not just be in your mind but in your heart and that it will prick your conscience to commit to acts of righteous faith. For a book and a faith *without works is dead.*

Amen.

Note

1. Paul Tillich, *Systematic Theology,* Vol. 3 (Chicago: The University of Chicago Press, 1976), 130.

CHAPTER SIX

A Conversation with the Community

Rodney T. Smothers

Since much of my ministry has been devoted to the planting of new congregations or the revitalization of existing congregations, much of my preaching has been centered on three primary themes: mission development, visioning, and witnessing. These share a common theological bond in their focus on God's intent for the church to be the vehicle through which people come into the knowledge of Christ as Savior and greatly influence my preaching agenda. My preaching focuses on the primary mission of the church, namely making disciples for Jesus Christ. This understanding of the salvation message and the importance of disciple-making has helped shape my preaching, which has evolved over the years to capture not only making disciples but also, more importantly, maturing disciples.

I believe that the most important things we do in the church are invite, transform, and send believers to attract, mature, and dispatch other believers into the world. Eugene Peterson, in The Message, puts it this way, "No prolonged infancies among us, please" (Ephesians 4:14). This has caused my preaching to change over time, and the evolution in my preaching has been shaped in my roles as pastor, Evangelism Director at the General Board of Discipleship, Adjunct Seminary Professor, Conference Director of Church Development, and guide for thirty-three congregations.

Preaching at its best leads believers to hear God's instructions regarding God's purpose for our lives. I understand the proclamation of the gospel to be compelling, confrontational, and covenantal in its scope, and the good news of the gospel sometimes comes in the midst of uncertain circumstances. This good news demands an encounter with God in our quest to find God in the midst of life's circumstances. Such an encounter may come as a gentle nudge that occurs at 4:00 a.m. and which leads me to a passage in the Bible that explodes with relevancy for the context of the sermon. At other times it may come as I consult the lectionary, my normal starting point, or as I listen for sermonic messages in the rhythms of life. Over the years I have developed series preaching as a pastoral discipline, so I tend to hear sermonic messages in ongoing stories. The seasons of the year and faithfulness to the theological themes of the liturgical season often shape the starting point of a preaching series, but the everyday encounters of living and the rhythms of congregational life may take over as the preaching series progresses.

I understand preaching to be a conversation with the community within and beyond the doors of the church. There are times when the preaching moment arrives and the Holy Spirit directs me in a completely different direction than the written manuscript. What I discern in reflection is that this action is not so much a departure from the prepared words but a God-directed message that the Holy Spirit wants preached in that moment. Since I preach multiple services each Sunday, no two messages are the same. The message for the congregation depends on the contextual connection that derives from the question: "In light of this, what would God have us do?"

Peace and justice are common and familiar issues when preaching to African Americans, who are impacted in every area of their lives because of race and culture. The Anglo congregation I serve in our Cooperative Parish is in as much need of God's transformative word but sometimes misses the influence that their privilege has upon their thinking. They have to be invited to think more about their role and responsibility as disciples of Jesus Christ instead of passing the needed work of transformation off to someone else. To keep the sermons in balance I generally use an outline or a manuscript. I use a manuscript when the subject matter needs to be precise, accurate, and specific to the context. And I use an outline when I am in my preferred teaching mode, because in this mode I usually am using a number of different scriptures to undergird the message. The outline permits me to walk around while preaching.

The type of sermon determines my style of preaching, and I prefer to wear vestments while I am preaching so that I have the freedom to be more expressive in my posture. My early memories of preaching were shaped in the Holiness tradition where there was little structure, and the preacher was very expressive, up close and personal. Seminary taught me the pros and cons of different styles of preaching. Experience has taught me to get a good feel of the preaching setting, sense how the Holy Spirit is moving, and move accordingly. What I have sought to discern is what best connects the preaching with the setting of the moment. Having preached in many different settings, my preaching is most formal with a high liturgical tradition and freest when moving in the prophetic tradition of laying on of hands and healing ministries.

Beyond my pastor, the Reverend E. W. Stevenson, and my mentor, the Reverend James Jacob Gray, the preacher who singularly influenced me most is James Forbes. This scholar-prophet somehow gave me permission to be multiple preachers and not allow myself to be limited to one style or form of delivery. What I most want the hearers of the sermon to walk away with is a clear understanding of what the gospel message invites us to do. I tend to lean more toward response than comfort, more toward doing than being, more toward learning than just hearing without action. Forbes's preaching allows all of these things to occur, and my experience of his preaching leaves me feeling as though I have had a nine-course meal. My hope for my own preaching is that by staying in the Word of God, I can expand my knowledge of the many dimensions of God, so that my preaching comes from the heart and not simply from the head.

The Stewardship of Leadership*
Isaiah 61:1-3

Just a few moments ago we installed the new leaders of this congregation for this year. The role of leadership is one that is so important and critical to the life of the congregation because as the leaders go, so goes the congregation. Our scripture texts, especially the passage from 1 Corinthians, help us understand what the roles and responsibilities of leadership involve. It speaks about unity and diversity in the body of Christ and reminds us that we are the people of God, gifted by God to serve one another; and helps to shape for us a mission statement for those who are called to lead God's people. The text from Isaiah identifies the seal of God's favor on those called to be leaders. Isaiah 61:1 says: "The spirit of the Lord...is upon me." This statement, and the focus of this message, presumes God's anointing upon those who would dare follow God's call to be leaders of God's people, and I would offer this morning that stewardship of that leadership role is the foundation through which and upon which our own understanding of call, context, culture, and commitment to serve must be based.

Today, as we affirm the selection of men and women who you, as a congregation, have selected to lead us as we move forward, they begin their tenure with an understanding that leadership is not just a title, it's a function. By definition, one who is a leader not only has followers but is involved in active participation in ministry, which is service. That service is possible only as those who lead do so with the anointing of the Spirit. I believe that needs clarification, so we need to unpack the dynamics of leadership.

First, leadership is about clarity of call. Every man, woman, boy, and girl has a call on their life from God, and part of the role of the ministry is to help people discern that call, to discover how it fits with other gifts in the life of the church, and to fully live in to that call. Not only that but at the end of the day our call shapes the way that we carry out our mission. In order to carry out our call we must develop our discipleship as followers of Christ and live into our commitment as disciples of Jesus Christ. Leaders must show up

* This sermon was preached at the 7:45 a.m. worship service at St. Paul UMC, Oxon Hill, Maryland, on January 9, 2011. View the preaching of this sermon on www.garrett.edu/styberg-bump/smothers

52

and be present so that as we see God's vision unfolding in our midst we can become co-laborers and help that vision to be realized as we become stewards of our leadership role.

Well, what does that mean? I believe that when we are entrusted to leadership it is not about us. It is about us understanding how God wants to use us. It really is about our discipleship, about the Spirit of God working in us. Jim Putman, in a book entitled *Real Life Discipleship: Building Churches That Make Disciples,* says that our first order of business is to create a leadership development factory. I love that term, a leadership development factory, because as a part of the body of Christ, one of the things we are challenged to do is to mature disciples for the work of ministry. In order to do that we must listen; we must learn; we must love; and we must launch. We begin as babes in Christ, become disciples of Christ, and then, through living out our discipleship, we become leaders in discipleship. Ultimately, we become multipliers of discipleship, which requires us to be stewards of our leadership role.

When we become stewards of leadership we see out of different lenses, and we begin to have different expectations. When we become stewards of leadership, the question is not what do I need but what does God require of me. When we become stewards of leadership, we begin to work not so much as an individual but we begin to seek opportunities to become a member of a team, a team of people working toward God-given goals, knowing that the Spirit of the Lord is on us. All of this is a part of the evolution of leadership. We as a congregation start by providing Christian instruction through our classes, our small groups, and other opportunities where people can gather together. Those small groups then develop into an accountable community where iron sharpens iron, where we come alongside one another and begin to say, "You know, that is a great idea." "Have you thought about this?" "Can we do this together?" or "Let's think through this as a team and ask ourselves is there a better way for us to accomplish this goal." All of this is deeply rooted in our understanding that what we are involved in is not our own. It's really not about us. It really is about God.

Discipleship is a team sport. Our scripture text invites us as a church, all of our ministries, into collaborative discernment. Why is that? We believe that the Spirit of God at work in the community through the leadership gives us a better outcome because we come together cooperatively and collectively to work together for the common good. We are not trying to work in silos. We are not trying to work as individual teams. We are not trying to talk about my budget and our program. Just the opposite is true. We are trying to find ways to bring things together so that we can move out together and make a strategic impact for the kingdom of God. You know what? That is hard work because that means we have to roll up our sleeves. We have to coordinate with one another. We have to stand back sometimes and let someone else take the lead, and we have to keep focus first and foremost on the things that God has called us to do. And we have to seek the anointing of the Holy Spirit.

"The Spirit of God is upon me." That means that God's anointing is resting upon each and every one of us. It means that whatever programs, whatever ministries, whatever strategies, whatever outreach that we do, we must continue to ask these questions: Does this take good news to the afflicted, does it bring hope to the brokenhearted, does it proclaim liberty to the captives, does it set prisoners free, does it announce the acceptable year of the Lord, does it announce the day of vengeance and justice, does it comfort those who mourn? All of these things become the foundational anchors of our priorities as a church. At the end of the day, all of our stewardship is focused on introducing people to an encounter with a saving God. No matter what we do. When we work with the schools, through the feeding programs, with the outreach arms of this church, those are just the expression of something much more meaningful. It is our way of connecting people in a relationship with Jesus Christ. And when we come together we must ask one another how we can extend this ministry of Christ beyond the physical doors of this church and make a greater impact in our community.

We in the church are God's representatives in the world. Rather than leaving church, when the sending forth is given today we should see ourselves as taking the church with us wherever we go. So if we are going to dinner at a fine restaurant or we are going to the movie or if we are going to the laundromat or if we are going to the library or if we are going to the mall, we are Christ's representatives because our call as leaders is not confined to a title, and the stewardship of leadership says that everywhere we go, we are held accountable as leaders of Christ's church to represent God in a way that honors God. It means that in all that we say and do each of us must show ourselves to be a follower of Christ, a disciple, to live up to our commitment of time, talent, gifts, service, and witness within and outside the church. God has entrusted much to our care, and we must be stewards of God's gifts and live into God's vision for the ministry and the vision of the kingdom of God in and for Christ's church.

Well, how will we get started? We all have to take a deep breath, hear in our hearts the message, "The Spirit of the Lord is upon me," and ask ourselves, "God, where would you have me to lead?" Remember, it is not about an office; it's really about a change of heart and mind. "God, where would you have me to lead?" I believe, brothers and sisters, that every one of you has a leadership season. Someone said to me, "Pastor, I don't know how to share my faith. I don't know how to testify. I don't know how to be a witness." I said, "Maybe those words are confusing you. Has God done anything for you?" They said, "Oh yeah!" I said, "Well, tell me your story." They started to tell their story and I said stop. They said, "I am not finished." and I said, "You have told me enough." They said, "What do you mean?" I said, "That is exactly what witnessing is about. That is exactly what a testimony is about. That is exactly what faith sharing is about. It is simply telling someone your story and how your relationship with Christ makes a difference each and every day." What's your story? How do you share the good news of the gospel with other people? How do you let people know you are a child of God?

Let me sound a note of caution right here: I know that there are some people who carry around the traveler's edition of the Bible tucked under their arms, and they are running down the streets with their fingers in the air, "You need to accept Jesus Christ as your Lord and Savior 'cause you are going to end up..." No, that's not what I am talking about. Sometimes you are just overhearing a conversation in the lunchroom at your job and you need to be a quiet presence and say, "Well, all that sounds good, but have you ever thought about this?" Sometimes you are in the line in the grocery store and somebody's complaining about this, that, and the other and you can say: "You know, I don't mean any harm, but have you ever thought about this?" Sometimes you are on the public transit on your way to and from and you hear somebody who is filled with despair: that's when the good news in you ought to leap out of you so that you can share with them that there is an answer to despair, there is hope in the midst of all of life's circumstances. When we become leaders in Christ then every day we seek opportunities to offer hope in the midst of despair through the Spirit of the Lord that is in you.

As we prepare to go forth from this place I want you to remember, leaders, there is a reason that Jesus sent his disciples out in twos. As you look around the congregation this morning you may wonder, "Who will do this with me?" But let us remember, as we seek to partner with others, that we are all about God's business and, as servants of God and leaders in the church, through the Spirit of God we can follow in the footsteps of Christ, who leads us all.

Let us pray:

Loving God, we are a team of people that you have blessed with a variety of gifts, talents, and abilities. By your Holy Spirit give us a spirit of unity and community as we strive to be stewards of all your gifts, especially the gift of leadership you have entrusted to us. So that in working together we may do so without competition, complaint, or comparison but walk alongside each other in mutual love, harmony, and care. Bless us as we go forth into this new year, and call us as a team of believers and servant-leaders to work together hand in hand, heart to heart, and to honor you in all that we say and do. These and all things we ask in Christ's name. Amen.

CHAPTER SEVEN

The Message in the Message

Telley Lynnette Gadson

God uses the preacher as a mouthpiece to share the good news of the gospel. That makes preaching a God-given gift to any individual who has been called to do the work of prophetic talk. Preaching is proclamation about salvation, deliverance, joy, and peace; and as a preacher I firmly believe that I am to walk in the spirit of accountability with proper study and preparation for the preaching moment. In preparing for the task, I am to also be in prayer and meditation that "the words of my mouth and the meditations of my heart" will be in line with the movement of God. I discern God's movement in the homiletical process to be one that is open enough to allow my voice to be heard, yet strong enough to keep the focus of the sermon on the message that God wants delivered to God's people.

I am clear that the preacher I was in 1992 is not the preacher I am today. My first sermon was preached on Sunday, November 29, 1992, as I served as the speaker for Student Day at my home church—Wesley United Methodist Church (Hollywood, South Carolina). The message was based on Romans 8:28-38 and entitled, "What's Your Persuasion." Even then I understood that the opportunity to preach the gospel is a blessed task. Over the years, my preaching has become more informed by the stretching of my faith in God and God's power to do more than I could ever imagine.

My seminary experience challenged my overall hermeneutic, thereby causing me to become more grounded in my understanding of what it means to preach. Over time, I have come to know that preaching is more than relaying written words from a manuscript to an audience; it is more than conveying thoughts from an outline; and it is more than practicing oratorical skills in the presence of a captive congregation. My homiletical theology has developed into a spiritual rapport between God and me, where I consecrate myself in the presence of God so that I am able not only to listen to what God is saying but also to get clarity as to how God wants me to relay the message. The Bible is filled with messages of help and hope, and the purpose of the message is to empower those who are willing to discern God's direction for life application of the good news.

My preaching is informed by the context of my culture and experience in society. My vantage point is that of an under-40, Black female from the Sea Islands of Charleston County in South Carolina, and the messages I bring touch the heart of real-life issues in such a way that people often remark, "I feel like you were telling my story." I am a product of the Black church experience; thus, I was raised in the preaching tradition of call and response. My delivery style is informed by my intention to engage the audience in the message, so in preaching I use movement—the movement of my hands, facial expressions, and sometimes full body gestures. The greatest influence on my delivery is my desire that the people get the message from the message. My preaching mentors have always reminded me that while it is a task to preach, it is an honor and a privilege to be God's mouthpiece.

Some of my learning in my "church and state" upbringing centered around the Christian's responsibility to actively participate in social justice issues that would bring peace on earth. I am comfortable speaking truth to power in the sermon as it relates to what happens beyond Sunday morning in our communities and in the world, and to ask questions like:

- How does our "shouting" on Sunday equip us to have success on Monday?
- Is the church making a difference in the community and challenging the status quo in order to participate in transformation, restoration, and elevation of all people?
- How does our faith intersect with the reality that present-day wars are hindering peace, and injustice often has more of a presence in the world than justice?

With me being the first hearer of my preaching, it is my hope that all the hearers are challenged, empowered, and committed to be better people to the glory of God.

There are preachers, past and present, who I admire and who have influenced my own preaching style, who have poured the wisdom of the ages into my life, thus impacting my preaching essence. My first mother in the ministry, the Reverend Angelin Jones Simmons, taught me that preaching is a lifestyle and it is important to walk in integrity. My first father in the ministry, the late Reverend Dr. Willis Timothy Goodwin, taught me to give all of myself to the preaching moment so that the people know that I have already been convicted and converted by the message. My childhood hairdresser, Pastor Joyce Marie Gordon, a preacher in the Holiness church, taught me about spiritual discipline. She believed that if you are going to talk the talk, you must walk the walk. My seminary professor and mother in homiletics, the Reverend Dr. Teresa Lynn Fry Brown, taught me the mechanics of the craft and held me accountable to "own and embrace" my voice in the preaching moment. I have been blessed by others who saw purpose, potential, and promise in my preaching: the Reverend Keith D. D. Lawrence, the Reverend Dr. Marion H. Newton, and the Reverend Dr. Ralph W. Canty.

What I like best about preaching is the energy I feel from those around me as I share messages of help, hope, and healing. What I love about preaching is knowing that God is willing to use me to do God's work of prophetic communication for such a time as this. My greatest challenge is making sure that the message is relevant for now, yet can still stand the best of changing times.

Stay in the Race*
Jeremiah 12:1-6

Do you know who I am? Have you heard the news? God has given me gifts and talents that I most certainly must use! So I stand before you today to proclaim God's word, understanding that we live in a world where many haven't heard. There is e-mail, hotmail, text to talk, and Yahoo too, but everybody hasn't read the memo that God can use anybody, everybody, somebody, and even a nobody to do something vibrant and new. The message is the same, the time is surely now, the method may be flavored with some hip-hop, but God still makes a way somehow. This is still the day that the Lord has made; we have reason to rejoice. Come on, sisters and brothers, let's give God our best praise with a loud voice! Good afternoon BMCR and praise the Lord!

I want to say to this body of believers that I am so thankful for the embrace of favor that I have received from many of you over these last eleven years that I have been serving in full-time pastoral ministry. You have been surrogate family to me, and that means a lot to an under-forty-year-old African American female pastor in The United Methodist Church. Each of these opportunities reminds me of what I once heard about how "being a young pastor is much like a roll of film; for in order to be developed, we must have exposure." So, thank you, BMCR, for this "Kodak moment" in ministry.

Here we are at this forty-third annual meeting of the organization that I affectionately call the NAACP of the UMC; here we are celebrating the journey of an organization, a caucus, a watch-group purposed to do justly, love mercy, and walk humbly in our time under God, which is surely now; here we are operating in an audacious spirit of putting P&W (praise and worship) in conversation with T-C-B (taking care of business); here we are speaking truth to power in the face of racism, sexism, classism, ageism, and personal-agenda-ism; and here we are pondering and processing our theme: Equipping the Saints for Ministry. The beauty of coming to a BMCR Meeting is that our culture lends itself to having you

---

* This sermon was preached at the forty-third annual meeting of National Black Methodists for Church Renewal held in 2010 in Jacksonville, Florida. View the preaching of this sermon on www.garrett.edu/styberg-bump/gadson

wonder are you at an annual conference or caught in a Tyler Perry drive-by, knowing that at any moment, the screen just might say, "Tyler Perry presents BMCR's Family Reunion starring Ronnie Miller-Yow, Jim Salley, Walter Kimbrough driving a Wells Fargo truck, and Cheryl Walker bringing up the rear passing out ballots for General and Jurisdictional Conference," or you just might hear the announcement that Vance Ross presents "The Diary of a Black Pastor's Convocation." I submit to you today that I come from a melting pot of dysfunction, of a father who is a functional alcoholic, a mother who is a functional evangelist, one brother who battles crack cocaine addiction and another who battles depression, and my obvious battle is obesity, yet I still choose to trust in the Lord until I die; and I admonish you to do the same.

Go with me, if you will, to the potter's house where all dysfunctions can be placed on the potter's wheel and we can become equipped to do the work of ministry, whether God calls us to be apostles, prophets, evangelists, pastors, or teachers. Now, turn to your neighbor and repeat after me: "Neighbor, equipping the saints for the work of ministry is not easy, but if we are going to be built up in unity and love for service, we must stay in the race."

I am sure that we can establish consensus that all of us have experienced times when we felt like life had given us sour grapes to eat or a bitter pill to swallow. When was the last time you visited a place where you "couldn't hear nobody pray," because you were caught between a rock and a few hard places? Can we tell the truth today that even when our faith has been at its best, we still have felt billows rolling and breakers dashing, trying to conquer our souls? Are there any pastors that are willing to admit that ministry is not always "going well" and the church is not always "growing by leaps and bounds"? Do we have any laity in the house who would admit that sometimes certain people want to hold the church hostage from growing because they are afraid that somebody will move their cheese of history and make them face their misery?

The prophet Jeremiah was all too familiar with these kinds of faith-community issues as he lived in response to God's call on his young life. Jeremiah, the son of Hilkiah, started a Harambe movement in his mother's womb and would later start a BMCR chapter in Judah petitioning God's people to repent of their disobedient ways, because destruction was sure to come. In his youth, God confirmed his call on Jeremiah's life and called him "a prophet to the nations"; however, Jeremiah was a good Methodist and he knew that the PPRC would have questions about his age. Jeremiah responds to God that he is only a child, and God responds to Jeremiah by telling him to eat the breakfast of champions, which is the word of God. God further tells this prophet to travel in the ministry race without fear because he would be covered by God's G-P-S (grace, purpose, and security).

Jeremiah's journey was the race of righteousness. On this race, he witnessed real-life experiences of sin and consequence, destruction and delusion, devastation and destitution, faults and failures, broken covenants and broken promises, ridiculous behavior and wrongful accusations, the young and restless, the old and tired, and everything in between; yet, this prophet witnessed God's power of protection and even God's gift of new mercy on a daily basis.

In chapter 12, we eavesdrop on Jeremiah's highly philosophical conversation with God. It is clear that Jeremiah has become well-acquainted with God's righteousness; however, he comes to God with concerns about God's justice. It seems that this Old Testament hip-hop preacher is facing a dilemma in his understanding, prompting him to ask the Lord: "Why does the way of the wicked prosper? Why do all the faithless live at ease? ... How long will the land lie parched and the grass in every field be withered" because of wickedness? (12:1, 4 NIV).

Jeremiah's questions are based on the issues, the isms and schisms that he encountered in the race of real life as a prophet. After facing persecution, opposition, and oppression for preaching truth to power with love, Jeremiah's humanity stands up, and he wants to know what does God plan to do about the ways of the wicked that are so clearly hindering the saints from being equipped, because many spoke God's name in the Temple but were quick to send a false god by the name of Baal a text message before leaving the worship service. To Jeremiah, this issue seemed to be an open-and-shut case that God should withhold mercy from the wicked and bless the faithful and obedient, who were doing their best to stay in the race. God allows Jeremiah to have his catharsis, because the Almighty recognized that this prophet had become a bit discouraged by the bad and the ugly and needed to be reminded that God called him to a purpose that is good.

In the final analysis, God gives Jeremiah points to ponder in the form of two questions: "If you have raced with [people] on foot and they have worn you out, how can you compete with horses? If you stumble in safe country, how will you manage in the thickets by the Jordan?" (12:5 NIV). God provides a teaching moment for Jeremiah, a teaching moment designed for this prophet to get the message that God is with him through the storms of life. God does not sugarcoat his response but rather wants Jeremiah to understand that the race "is what it is" and in the race, there will be these difficult times and times of even greater difficulty, but God has made this prophet a promise to protect him and to elevate him to a place where he will face great challenges but even greater protection. God even gives Jeremiah a tip to stay in the race by telling him that people who speak well of you may also transform into those who speak against you, so do not trust them, even if they are as close as family. God wants Jeremiah to stay in the race.

I am confident that each of us has played the role of Jeremiah at some point in our own lives. Whether we are clergy or laity, we know that God has called us to the work of service so that the body of Christ can be built up with faith, hope, and love, working to become more mature each day so that we have the power to stay in the race. Staying in the race doesn't mean that you will be the fastest or go the longest distance, but if you stay in God's race, you will make it to the finish line that has been ordained for your life. If you stay in God's race, you will be equipped with race-wear to run with horses and make the best of life even if you have to walk through the thickets of the Jordan.

While we are staying with God in the race of life, we will meet others who look like they are on our team, but they are really caught up in other agendas. These racers have praise on their lips but nothing in their hearts. These racers treat the church more like a social club for intellectually elite rather than a hospital for sinners. These racers say they are equipping the saints, but they are not familiar with the owner's manual. These racers have position but no power. These racers have prestige but no purpose. These racers have money but no mission. These racers have degrees but no depth for duty. These racers have religion but no relationship.

These racers have appointment but no anointing. These racers have status but haven't sold out to the Savior. My sisters and brothers, as I encourage you, I am encouraging myself to stay in the race that God has marked out for us. In order to stay in this race and not become consumed by any other race, we must do three important things: pray, stay focused, and never give up.

First, we must pray. When we hear God's voice calling us to do God's will and when we are willing to listen to divine instruction, our prayer life becomes even more powerful because it is then that we learn how to pray and what to pray for. So many times, we just up and do what we want to do and expect God to co-sign our actions as if we are doing God a favor. When we spend time praying that God will reveal what God has planned for our lives, we will grow in knowledge and maturity. A constant and abiding prayer life will keep us in the race, and even when the race becomes difficult, the lessons will make us better and not bitter.

Second, we must stay focused. Once we are clear as to what God wants us to do in the race of righteousness, we must keep our eyes on the prize, which is to help equip others to participate in the race. It is the devil's job to take our focus off of the big picture that is connected to a ministry mindset, so that our vision becomes dilated by the miniscule and mundane, the small stuff that does nothing to help equip the saints but gratifies "the ain'ts," those who ain't doing nothing in the church, ain't doing nothing in the community, ain't praying for the pastor, ain't paying tithes and offerings, ain't doing anything positive or productive to build up the body of Christ.

Third and finally, in order to stay in the race, we must be determined to never give up. A commitment to prayer and the tenacity to stay focused are the key ingredients to a never-give-up mentality. We don't have to wait until someone says that they will support us, we don't have to wait until the choir sings our favorite song, we don't have to wait until the storm passes over—our time under God is now. And if we are determined to never give up, if we are determined to stay in the race, we can praise God "on credit," knowing that we are going to win the race. If we never give up, we can race with people on two feet and horses on four legs; if we never give up, we can see God's hand moving in every jurisdiction and across the denomination; if we never give up, we don't have to spend time worrying about the next great appointment or who looks like they are running ahead of us. That ain't your job; your job is to stay in the race. And furthermore, the Bible says, "The race is not given to the swift nor is the battle given to the strong" (Ecclesiastes 9:11, paraphrased). So we must stay in the race. Stay in the race and watch God move. Even when you get mixed messages from people who act like they want to celebrate you but they really just tolerate you, you will do better in the race if you pronounce a benediction on those kinds of people: May the Lord watch between me and thee because we need to be absent, one from another.

Stay in the race. As you pray, stay focused and never give up. You will need to be encouraged in this race. To be encouraged, you've got to know how to spell race: **R-A-C-E**. With these letters, you can throw your own pep rally! Come on, somebody,

Give me an **"R"**

  Give me an **"A"**

    Give me a **"C"**

      Give me an **"E"**

"R"—we are Redeemed, Recovered, Restored, Righteous.

"A"—we are Available, Ambitious, Anointed, Able.

"C"—we are Covered, Christ-centered, Co-laboring, Competent.

"E"—we are Enthusiastic, Edified, Empowered, Effective.

Let's have a pep rally and take this thing on home. Come on, everybody, give me an "R," give me an "A," give me a "C," give me an "E," and say after me:

I'm a Radical Advocate for Civil Engagement!

I'm Ready to be Advanced in my Character and Excellence!

And I will **STAY IN THE RACE**!

And now unto him who is able to keep me from falling, to the only One who can keep us in the race, be all glory, all honor, and all power; from this time forth and forevermore...SAY YEAH!

CHAPTER EIGHT

A Means of Grace

Tracy Smith Malone

The preaching moment is more than just another element of the worship service. I believe it is the central act of worship—the main event. Preaching is a means of grace that bears witness to the extravagant love of God. It celebrates the hope and life we have in Christ Jesus. Preaching is the manifestation of God being made flesh to dwell among us. When the Scriptures are proclaimed, the power of God is present among us, speaking and meeting us in our present circumstances and calling us into a new future with hope. Preaching also edifies and transforms the hearers, moving them toward making changes in their personal lives and toward making a difference for Christ in the world.

Over the years I have discovered that preaching is most effective when you know the souls of who you are in dialogue with or the context in which you are preaching. The sermon has the potential to be more relevant and far-reaching when the preacher is aware of the hearers' doubts, pain, fears, struggles, and the situations in their lives—be it family, society, or national or world events. The preacher must take account of all the things that influence the hearers, and allow the sermon to speak God's word into their situation. In the preaching moment, the Holy Spirit intercedes, helping the preacher and hearer know the mind of Christ, and reveals what God wants them to be and do.

This revelation does not happen without much prayer and preparation. The preacher must take time to carefully study the biblical text and plan the sermonic moment. I think it is important to determine the scripture, the style, and the format. If I am addressing a particular issue that exists in society or a major crisis that has emerged, I choose to preach a topical sermon and search the Scriptures to find a relevant text. If I am preaching the Revised Common Lectionary, which is common for me, I tend to preach expository sermons. Whether topical or expository, they both require intentional preparation.

My preparation begins a week before I am to preach. I read and pray over the Scriptures every day. I look for the surprise in the text—that which is not obvious. I take notes each time I re-read the text. Mid-week I consider other resources: biblical commentaries, relevant stories, personal encounters, societal conditions. I then develop an outline and begin to shape the sermon. The sermon continues to be shaped up to the moment that it is being preached. Even then I am still listening so that I might preach the wisdom of God. That is essential because I believe that in the preaching event God is being made flesh to dwell among us. As scripture declares, "Whoever listens to you listens to me" (Luke 10:16).

I prefer to use a manuscript for preaching; however, it does not serve as a crutch. It simply keeps me focused and allows me to make the most use of the metaphors and images that are part of my poetic style. There is a rhythmic element to my style of preaching that helps make the words come alive to the hearers. I preach primarily from the pulpit but often walk among the people, especially when sharing a story or singing my prayers. I trust the Holy Spirit to guide my steps when I am leading worship. I have been told by many that I am a passionate preacher, and I hold this affirmation to be true because I believe that the Word of God should be preached with passion and power. Sermon delivery is just as important as the sermon content. The preacher is God's messenger, and we have the responsibility to be the channel through which God's message is heard. The message takes on the risk of losing its potency if it is not preached with zeal.

Passionate preaching is primary for the strengthening and building up of the body of Christ. While growing up in the church I was exposed to both dynamic, prophetic preaching and the kind of preaching that lacked preparation and was poorly delivered. I've witnessed the amazing discipleship that takes place when the preaching is relevant and informed. And I've seen the damage preaching has done to individuals and congregations when the preacher had lost the sacredness and integrity of the preaching moment. My intention is always to encourage the hearers to receive the sermon as a source of strength and a beacon of hope as they meet the challenges of their lives.

I really enjoy preaching and often find that it is difficult to balance the time between my weekly pastoral duties and sermon preparation. What I love most about preaching is telling and retelling the story of how God loves us with an everlasting love. I enjoy recounting the acts of God's goodness and mercy and God's calling on us to work for peace and justice. And it gives me great joy to proclaim that God's spirit is ever at work transforming the world and making all things new. And because I know that the preaching moment is central to one's life and faith, and I feel I have an obligation to give God and God's hearers my best, sermon preparation is a priority in my ministry. My time of preparation is time with God as I listen for what God wants for God's people as God invites us to participate in kingdom building.

What I hope to always accomplish in the preaching event is to convince the hearers that while we are seeking God, our great God in Christ is seeking to transform us and the entire world. We are the hands and the feet of Christ, and the sermon gives voice to God's transforming presence recorded in scripture and alive in the hearts of the people. By delivering God's word to the people, the preacher becomes God's agent of justice, peace, and hope in the world.

Embracing Who We Are[*]
Matthew 5:13-20

Our Gospel lesson this morning is one of the greatest compliments that has ever been given to the body of Christ, individually and collectively: "You are the salt of the earth. You are the light of the world. You are a city set upon a hill."

Being characterized as "salt and light" and as a "city set upon a hill" is honorable and humbling and yet very complicated and challenging. These are some big shoes to fill. This declaration and call on our lives is not a question about who we should become or simple attributes that we might someday obtain. It is a matter of who we already are.

"You are the salt of the earth. You are the light of the world. You are a city set upon a hill." Embrace who you are!

These words of affirmation are used to describe who Christ's followers are and what they are called to be and do in the world.

When Jesus gave his Sermon on the Mount, which includes this passage of scripture, he was speaking to his disciples and the crowd that gathered among them. This was a message that was not just about ethical and principled rules for living; he was addressing a people who were in exile. The Roman Empire had occupied Israel's land. Even though the people of Israel had physically returned to the land, the exile continued. The land, the city, and the Temple were still being ruled by the Roman Empire. They began to raise complicated questions, as we do when we cannot see or understand where God is at work: Why is this happening to us? Does God not care about us? What does God want us to do? How do we respond?

These questions and fears caused division and anxiety among the people of Israel. Jesus preached this Sermon on the Mount to encourage Israel to remember who they were. He wanted them to not withdraw and resign in fear and disillusionment, only being concerned about their personal spiritual well-being and preserving their own lives. Instead, they were being reminded that they were called to be a holy nation—a people of moral principle. They were a

[*] This sermon was preached at the Gary UMC in Wheaton, Illinois, on February 6, 2011. View the preaching of this sermon on www.garrett.edu/styberg-bump/malone

community of faith that was being called to act justly and to love mercy while walking humbly with their God. They were to be a voice for the voiceless, concerned about the plight of others, and not become comfortable with the status quo. Jesus said, "You are the salt of the earth. You are the light of the world. You are a city set upon a hill." In other words, embrace who you are!

In remembering who they were, they were challenged to not hate and resist their enemies but to love and pray for them. They were to confront the empire, proclaiming and living out God's justice! And to know that God was already doing a new thing! Like Israel, if we are the salt of the earth and the light of the world, how then are we to live? How are we to confront the empire in which we live?

Let's take a look at this metaphor, salt. Salt is used to alter or enhance food. It makes food come alive by bringing out the best flavors. Salt is used as a preservative—keeping food fresh for a period of time. Salt is also used to melt away ice on the ground, making the path safe and secure. What about light? Light enables us to see things that we would otherwise not see so clearly if at all. Light is energy that gives things color. It provides solar power for electricity. Light at night can be seen for miles.

As followers of Christ, we are to have an antiseptic influence on life, seeking ways to break down the barriers that separate us one from another. We are to be beacons of light in those places where darkness triumphs over hope. Our faithfulness and our works ought to encourage others to do good. As a community of faith we are to reflect God's light so that all people and nations can know and experience God's justice and mercy. By the grace of God, we are called to preserve healthy relationships, work for peace, repair brokenness in community, encourage diversity, and represent hope.

Embrace who you are!

I find it rather curious that Jesus says, "If the salt loses its saltiness, how can it be made salty again? It is no longer good for anything, except to be thrown out and trampled" underfoot (Matthew 5:13 NIV). One might say that salt cannot lose its flavor. Could it possibly be that salt can lose its flavor if it stops being salt or lacks purity? Perhaps Jesus is saying to us that if we are not faithful in being salt and light, channels of love and doers of justice, it is as if we have stopped being ourselves. And that does the world no good. Our identity, our faith in Christ, our discipleship will then serve no greater purpose than that of our own selfish desires.

"A city on a hill cannot be hidden. Neither do people light a lamp and put it under a bowl. Instead they put it on its stand, and it gives light to everyone in the house" (Matthew 5:14-15 NIV). The question is: How are you being salt and light?

Embrace who you are!

We are called to live for Christ. It's that simple and that difficult. For Jesus did not come to lead us out of this world but to show us how to live in it. What a challenge! What an opportunity!

I can remember hearing a story told about Martin Luther, the great Protestant reformer, regarding his ministry and the challenges he faced. When he felt discouraged and overwhelmed with the troubles of his times, he would touch his forehead and say to himself, "Martin, be calm, you are baptized!"

In these times of great challenge, doubt, inner turmoil, hopelessness, anxiety, and fear of being who we are called to be, we can do like Martin Luther. We can touch our foreheads, remember who we are, and say, "I am the salt of the earth. I am the light of the world. I am a city built upon a hill." You see, the Christian message is not that we have to try to act like salt and light. The Christian message is "we are salt and light." It is a matter of embracing who we are! It is a matter of being who we are called to be, right here and right now.

As followers of Christ, we cannot rest as long as even one of God's own is in misery, hungry, naked, oppressed, persecuted, or disenfranchised. We cannot rest as long as any institution or system causes harm and misrepresents God's righteousness and justice.

Embrace who you are!

Many find themselves asking questions, "How does the church respond to this call?" "How do we become the salt and the light?" Many churches find themselves busying themselves trying to address what the need happens to be at the time. Perhaps the answer lies in faithful living of the great commission: "Go ye therefore into all the world preaching the good news and baptizing them in the name of the Father, Son, and Holy Spirit" (Matthew 28:19, paraphrased). Perhaps the task of the church is to help the world to discover its true identity as God's world. "God is love and

whoever abides in love abides in God and God abides in them"
(1 John 4:16, paraphrased).

Embracing who we are is a challenge even for the most faithful
among us. Marianne Williamson addresses this challenge in her
book *Return to Love*. She writes:

> Our deepest fear is not that we are inadequate. Our deepest fear
> is that we are powerful beyond measure. It is our light, not our
> darkness, that most frightens us. We ask ourselves, who am I to
> be brilliant, beautiful, talented and fabulous? Actually, who are
> you not to be? You are a child of God. Your playing small doesn't
> serve the world. There's nothing enlightened about shrinking so
> that other people won't feel insecure around you. We were born
> to make manifest the glory of God that is within us. It's not just in
> some of us. It's in everyone. And as we let our lights shine, we
> unconsciously give other people permission to do the same. As
> we are liberated from our own fear, our presence liberates others.[1]

Not everyone has the moral strength to be "light and salt" or a
"city built upon a hill." It takes spiritual courage to take a stand or
to do what is right, knowing that you might be standing by yourself. When we let our light shine, we encourage others to let their
light shine as well. The message we model is that we always do the
right thing because it is the right and just thing to do.

Jesus tells his followers that they are light of the world and that
this light should not be hidden but seen by all. Someone has well
said, there can be no such thing as secret discipleship, for either the
secrecy destroys the discipleship or the discipleship destroys the
secrecy. Christianity is meant to be seen and to be evident to all.

It should be seen in major ways as we work for justice and advocate for peace; but also even in the simplest of ways. It should be
seen in how we interact with our co-workers, interact with our
neighbors, socialize with our friends, have conversation among
our circles, in the way we treat those who serve us at the local
restaurant, grocery store, or coffee shop, on the golf course and basketball court. And even the way we drive.

William Sloane Coffin, one of the greatest preachers of our time,
says it this way:

> There is no way that Christianity can be spiritually redemptive
> without being socially responsible. A Christian cannot have a

personal conversion experience without experiencing at the same time a change in social attitude. Jesus said what you have done unto the least of these.... God is always trying to make humanity more human. But without us he won't, just as without him we can't.[2]

Every time we raise questions asking how long will evil prevail, violence run rampant, corruption exist, forms of exclusion exist, we can be sure that God is asking the same questions of us. Our calling to be salt and light is to help God protect and dignify life. We partner with God as we affirm the worth of all hues of humanity. Christ is God's love personified, and the church is God's love organized. Every church, every believer's calling, characterizes a love that seeks direction and form. And what defines the church is not our social principles or faith and doctrinal standards but the integrity of our love.

William Temple says, "The church is the only organization that exists for those who are not its members." The church exists to make manifest the love of God and to bring people into relationship with God's extraordinary love. Therefore we should not resign to make our peace with the world's madness. It is all too easy to become cynical and settle by saying this is just how things are.

We must be the "salt and light" in the spaces and places we occupy. We must be willing to go into the darkness that exists and confront it with God's love and justice. We must be bringers of hope. Desmond Tutu, in a 1992 interview with *Christianity Today* magazine, was asked if he was hopeful about the future. "I am always hopeful," he replied. "A Christian is a prisoner of hope. What could have looked more hopeless than Good Friday? There is no situation from which God cannot extract good."

Remember, Christ has no eyes but ours, no hands but ours, no feet but ours. Embrace who you are! "You are the salt of the earth. You are the light of the world. You are a city built upon a hill."

Notes

1. Marianne Williamson, *A Return to Love* (San Francisco: Haper Paperbacks, 1992), 165.

2. William Sloane Coffin, *The Collected Sermons of William Sloane Coffin: The Riverside Years*, Vol. 1 (Louisville: Westminster John Knox Press, 2008).

CHAPTER NINE

A Timeless Message of Love

Leo W. Curry

Theologically, I believe that the sermon should teach, illuminate, and inspire. In preaching, we point specifically to Jesus Christ as the center of our faith and we look intentionally at the life, ministry, and teachings of Jesus to determine what his example means for us, in the present age. I want each sermon to challenge the hearers with the question: "Are we feeble Christians or faithful disciples?" I pray throughout the week to discern God's movement in the homiletical process, that the sermon will be all about God revealed in Christ Jesus our Lord.

The guiding principle for me is that the message must be Christocentric, that it should faithfully portray Christ's life and teachings and lead to a better understanding of Christ's demands on our lives as faithful disciples. The sermon is not about me, nor is it all about the hearers, so I am really concerned that it will contribute in some way to the development in discipleship of the hearers. What I preach should help them grow to fullness, maturity, and stature in Christ Jesus. I hope that because of the message that I preach, they will truly love God more dearly and appropriate more fully what it means to be a faithful disciple of Christ in this present age.

Preaching gives us the opportunity to offer a timeless message of God's steadfast love and grace incarnate in Jesus Christ, who was, who is, and who is to be. Although each event of preaching takes place in a particular time and place, and the content of the good news is being proclaimed to a particular people, God is in control regardless of the time. The good news of the gospel must be proclaimed in every sermon. The sermon should remind the hearers of a God of grace, a God of many second chances, a God of love who did not send the Son to condemn but to save, a God who desires that all should come to repentance.

However, along with that good news, a well-constructed sermon aims to confront, challenge, or admonish when necessary. The impact of our culture and society on sermons must always be viewed through the lens of Christ's teachings, especially his inaugural sermon in Luke's Gospel (Luke 4:16-19) and Jesus' teachings of the kingdom of God. Living in the kingdom of God, the tension between the already and the not yet makes one confront issues of peace and justice. The "isms" of our present age, which do not promote or produce peace and justice for all of God's children, are appropriate sermon content, since the task of the preacher is to be prophetic in the name of and for the sake of Jesus Christ. In fact, any issue, movement, or fad that excludes rather than includes is fodder for the sermon content. The caveat is that not every whim or fad in society needs to be treated in every sermon.

What I like best about preaching is that through each sermon God grants the people and the preacher another opportunity to grow, to learn, and to be transformed into the fully developed human beings God intends us to be. Preaching a sermon each week offers another chance to try to grasp what God in Christ is saying to us, calling us to become, and telling us so that we can understand what we are to do as Christians and disciples of Jesus Christ. It requires the preacher to present the good news with integrity and faithfulness to one's call. What makes this challenging is that too often people wish to have a soothsayer or entertainer in the pulpit on Sunday morning. Many claim to desire solid biblical preaching but can become cantankerous or contentious when it is offered.

Using the lectionary for each Sunday's sermon requires me to be disciplined about the preaching task. I spend a significant amount of time in preparation for preaching because I find that sermon preparation requires extensive reading of a variety of materials, not just the Bible. I use several resources weekly that focus on the lectionary, and I find living with the texts throughout the week to be indispensable. I keep pen and paper on my nightstand and sometimes I wake up and jot down ideas that come to me. I pray each week that the sermon will be a fragrant offering to God and a spiritual benefit to both people and pastor. Similar to the lectionary, using a manuscript is a discipline. It is also a reminder of the preparation that is required in order to prepare and equip God's people for living as Christ's disciples.

My sermons are generally expository because of my conviction that the people must not only hear the good news but also learn something each week about the content of the faith, the Bible, and the demands of discipleship. There is a story to tell based upon the biblical narratives, and for me the exposition is key. In my estimation, topical sermons can be a two-edged sword. They can sometimes be used for the pastor's personal agenda, a gripe session, or a favorite issue or cause, which may not resonate with the people or offer the good news in a meaningful way. On the other hand, some occasions require a topical sermon, such as the events of September 11, 2001. Regardless of style, I am careful about crafting the sermon so that it is accessible to all hearers.

I learned that most important lesson from my mentor, the late Reverend Edward D. McGowan, who was hailed as "a prince of preachers." Having listened to him for a number of years impels me to give as much time and attention as possible to developing the content of each sermon, and to delivering the sermon in a way that allows the message of Christ to be heard. The appropriate use of stories or illustrations, and the need to be careful about projection, diction, and enunciation are as critical as the proper selection and interpretation of scripture, but above all it is the message of God's grace through Christ that makes the sermon worthy of preaching.

What God Tells Us: Imitate!*
Matthew 5:38-48

This morning as we look at our scripture lessons from 1 Corinthians and the Gospel of Matthew, we do well to observe and recognize that we live in a world which has its own folk wisdom and treasured sayings which a good number of us believe and endorse, both consciously and unconsciously. Although the apostle Paul proclaims in 1 Corinthians 3:19: "For the wisdom of this world is foolishness with God. For it is written, 'He catches the wise in their own craftiness'; and again, 'The LORD knows the thoughts of the wise, that they are futile'" (NKJV), these are words which do not flow off the tongue as fleetingly as some of our more popular sayings from folk wisdom.

I know what Paul says, but sometimes you just have to practice tit for tat. Of course, we teach this quite early to our children. If somebody hits you at school or on the playground, you'd better hit him or her back. Don't come crying home to me or I'll hit you myself. You can't be soft in this world. Otherwise, people will walk all over you.

Frequently and sadly, some of us adhere to the "don't get mad, get even" school of wisdom. This view advocates: "Do unto others as they do unto you." You have to even things up. Some go even further and say: "Don't get mad, annihilate."

Thus, again today we are confronted with our continuing theme and its variations: What God Tells Us. By now some of us may be pretty much out of joint with what Jesus tells us in all of his teachings in the Sermon on the Mount in this fifth chapter of Mathew's Gospel. Last week we noted that what Jesus tells us is to choose. Choose well how we handle issues of murder, anger, contempt, reconciliation, lust, and adultery.

Today's Gospel lesson is Mathew's conclusion of the antithesis section of the Sermon on the Mount. Here Jesus contrasts the previously held view of the Law with the new interpretation he brings. And, dear friends, what Jesus tells us in this conclusion to the Sermon on the Mount is imitate. Imitate me. Imitate my way. Imitate God's way that it is my task to reveal to you.

* This sermon was preached at the Fordham UMC in Bronx, New York, on February 20, 2011. View the preaching of this sermon on www.garrett.edu/styberg-bump/curry

Jesus uses again these words: "You have heard that it was *said*, but *I say* to you." An eye for an eye and a tooth for a tooth. Although the Law was intended to limit or curtail excessive acts of retaliation or punishment, in too many instances, with the tacit approval of the religious authorities, incidents of increasing violence and personal vendettas escalated.

What Jesus teaches is: no pay back, no getting even, no tit for tat, not even the stony silent treatment which some are prone to use. When Jesus says, "Do not resist an evildoer," he is telling us in trying to get revenge or pay back an evildoer, we ourselves might just *become* the very evil we so vehemently oppose.

We are called to participate with Christ in building the Kingdom and in his ministry of reconciliation. We are also called to imitate Christ. Christ's life is the very embodiment of not seeking tit for tat or revenge. Christ was lied about. He was tortured. He was crucified.

Consider that the response to a slap on the right cheek is to "turn the other also" (Matthew 5:39). When someone is struck on the right side of the face, it is a backhanded blow delivered by someone with authority to someone lacking in authority. Such a backhanded slap is really more insult than injury—a slap delivered by a master to a slave, a landowner to a sharecropper, and in some cases an angry parent to an unruly child. Yet to turn the other or left cheek would mean that you are placing yourself on equal footing with the aggressor. Now, your would-be aggressor must use the fist of his right hand to strike again. To hit someone with the fist means the other person is an equal. So when you turn the other cheek, the aggressor's power to dehumanize and oppress is counteracted or removed.

Let's look at the coat and cloak scene. In the first century, the average Jewish man wore two pieces of clothing. He wore a tunic of linen and wool next to his body, with a heavier outer cloak. His outer cloak frequently served as a blanket as well. This outer cloak was covered by the Law. It could not be demanded as collateral or security for a loan. In the case of a possible lawsuit portrayed here, in which the debtor is forced to give up both his coat and cloak, it would be utterly scandalous. Being in debt was fairly common for the first-century Jews suffering under the weight of the oppressive Roman occupation with gouging taxes. To give up both coat and cloak would make the defendant naked. Since it was utterly shameful to look at another person naked, the creditor would naturally bring shame upon himself.

The verse which says, "If anyone forces you to go one mile, go also the second mile" (5:41), refers to the legal right of the occupying Roman army to make any citizen serve as their personal porter. Jesus instructs: "Do not resist; offer to go the extra mile." Why? The Roman law said that the soldier could make the civilian carry his baggage for only one mile. Anything more than a mile subjected the soldier to disciplinary action. Thus Jesus is offering the oppressed a liberating way to protest a hated law and the possibility of the aggressive oppressor getting a reprimand.

We do well today to look also with some intentionality at the verse which tells us, "Give to everyone who begs from you," and "Do not refuse anyone who wants to borrow from you" (5:42). I am the first to confess that this is difficult. What it means is that in our current world of great economic inequity, where the rich have gotten richer, and where the rich with the help of some politicians are doing everything to get even richer, and with virulent vitriolic attacks on the working classes and the least of these, the grossly uneven distribution of wealth widens: Jesus says: "Give, and don't refuse."

What this truly signifies is that we are called to put others first. We are called to regard the needs of others as more important than the needs of our own. We are called to follow and imitate Christ with high personal cost that is *financial*. Jesus seems to tell us this sharing is one of the ways to alleviate poverty and restore human dignity. For those among us who may be thinking: "Well, doesn't the Bible say that charity begins at home?" I'm afraid that I must share that this tidbit of folk wisdom is attributed to Benjamin Franklin and not found in the Bible.

The final portion of what Jesus tells us in today's Gospel focuses on the radical nature of our love of neighbor. "Love your enemies and pray for those who persecute you" (5:44). This too is a particularly demanding challenge even for pastors in 2011. We pastors are open to harsh criticisms and attacks; we may even make some enemies when we mention money. We can repeat countless times that giving in the church is not a money problem but a spiritual problem. It is a question of priorities in our modern-day world. We are going to have enough money for the hair, the nails, the cell phone, the cable or Direct TV payment, the car payment on the upscale gas guzzling car, and to grab a quick bite from one of the many fast food joints we don't need. Pastors get it when they imitate Christ by telling biblical truths.

One article this past summer highlighted the depression that pastors are prone to because parishioners don't want to grow spiritually or to change. They want the pastor to soothe, to entertain, to care for them. When the pastor is fulfilling all the pastoral and priestly roles, everything is hunky-dory. When the pastor proclaims the prophetic work of God, as Jesus tells it in today's Gospel, he or she may encounter enemies within the church who make up stuff, who falsely accuse and delight in telling abusive lies. Yet to both pastor and people, Jesus says this day: "Love your enemies and pray for those who persecute you."

Just as God the Father gives sunshine and rain to the righteous and unrighteous, we are called as followers of Christ—those who earnestly strive to be devotedly faithful followers—we are called to imitate Christ and demonstrate unqualified love for *all*, including *enemies*. Even tax collectors and Gentiles love those who love them in return. We, as followers of Jesus, are called to do more. Above all, discipleship is defined as love that goes beyond what is required. Turning the other cheek, giving your cloak, going the extra mile, and giving generously are all expressions of the extravagant love we are to give even to our enemies.

Let us observe also that today's Gospel lesson is appropriate for the observance of Black History Month. Jesus is the preeminent Teacher and Model for the Civil Rights Movement. He instructs the oppressed and disenfranchised in how to resist and protest the yoke of Roman oppression. What Jesus teaches is not just a complete rupture with the *modus operandi* of the day or accepted status quo, but he teaches what Gandhi and Dr. Martin Luther King, Jr., later used in their struggles for liberty and freedom—passive resistance, or the nonviolent means against injustice, which undergirded the Civil Rights Movement.

Oh, dear friends, Jesus tells us to imitate him and the heavenly Father. "Be perfect, therefore, as your heavenly Father is perfect" (5:48). Please rest assured that this is not a call to a life free from sin. That is both literally and virtually impossible for all of us. "Be perfect, as your heavenly Father is" means to practice and exhibit the same love, mercy, grace, compassion, and justice that God has for all of us—far beyond our deserving. Does this sound too lofty or humanly impossible to imitate our God in Jesus Christ this way? The good news is, because our God does not deal with us tit for tat; does not retaliate (as we deserve); always provides both the cloak and coat for our protection; goes the second mile with us; loves us all, both friends and his foes; and causes the sun to rise on the evil and the good, the rain to fall on the righteous and the unrighteous, we then can imitate God, because God gives us the power, the means, and the example of Jesus step by step along our pilgrim journey. What God tells us is imitate; imitate me. And indeed God, and God alone, enables us to do so. Thanks be to God.

In the name of the Father, the Son, and the Holy Spirit. Amen.

CHAPTER TEN

The Privilege of a Divine Gift

Rose Booker-Jones

Preaching is an artistic gift of God that summons all people to a covenant of love that offers salvation. It is a gift of God that loves, saves, heals, encourages, comforts, and gives hope to a people whom God loves. Preaching, through the power of the Holy Spirit, is a balm that soothes the wounded, mends the broken, and comforts the despised. God chose to impart this gift of preaching to human beings so that they might hear or otherwise experience the love of God for humanity. As individuals we are called and sent to preach God's message of salvation and hope to those who have not believed and those who have not heard.

Personally for me this was a hard call to receive. Raised in an environment of male preachers, the ideology of a woman doing more than preparing the elements for the Sacrament of Holy Communion was unheard of. God calling me to preach had to be a figment of my imagination. It wasn't until the call became so powerful and passionate that it finally dawned on me: "God's talking to me! God is calling me!" So to read in the apostle Paul's letter the words of Isaiah's prophecy with reference to preachers: "How beautiful are the feet of those who bring good news!" (Romans 10:15c) helped me to see my call as a humbling privilege and a gift of God.

In preparation for preaching the good news of Jesus Christ I've learned to focus first on the One who called me to this task. So I pray. Prayer is a continual portion of my life. You could say it's the portion of my strength. Prayer! Not just prayer during a time of devotion but a continual conversation with God throughout the day. Sermon topics or ideas flood my thoughts at the office, in conversation with others, or driving to my next appointment. I have to confess, even during meetings a sermon topic or scripture text will come to mind. So I inconspicuously try to jot down my thoughts without anyone noticing, hoping they just think I'm taking notes; all the while in my spirit I'm talking with God. And let's not forget the countless number of 3 a.m. impromptu meetings with God about the next sermon series. Prayer!

While I may find the lectionary useful during the special seasons of the church such as Advent, Christmas, Lent, and Easter, generally, I select the scripture text for preaching based on a sermon topic or series, then exegete the text with a topic in mind. I have a Bible in one hand and the newspaper (CNN) in the other hand, sometimes literally. This is important! Speaking to the needs of the church community is vital to bringing them closer to Christ. Therefore, I read the text with others in heart. I always keep in mind that someone may be worshiping for the first time, so I consider what word would win them to Christ. Or someone may be dealing with issues beyond their scope of understanding, so I ask myself, what word can I share that will bring them closer to God? As preachers we must be careful about the message we deliver. Our words can empower as well as condemn; heal as well as wound. Preachers should be in the business of lifting or pointing people toward God. Justice flows like a river and peace floods the soul when sermons direct individuals to God's saving power in Jesus Christ that sets us free. As I prepare to preach I ponder many questions: "How will this message lift up? How will this message lead to healing? Who will it help set free? How will they believe?"

Next in sermon preparation is laying everything out in manuscript. I choose to use a manuscript because of my stance in staying on topic. I believe that people are able to follow a message that starts and ends with a particular theme or subject. It also helps them retain and carry the message to family or friends. The manuscript also gives me a place to record research, give statistics, or recount stories. I often quote pastors, theologians, or scholars on subject matter. So preaching by manuscript has been my tool of choice throughout my ministry. However, a manuscript may restrict you to the pulpit, so toward the end of the sermon—the celebration—I intentionally move from the pulpit and walk around. At Perkins School of Theology, Professor Zan Holmes taught that every sermon should end with a celebration—celebrating God's love and plan of salvation through Christ Jesus. During the celebration I walk around, interacting with and connecting with the people.

I recall during my first two years of preaching I tried to sound like a man by lowering my voice (now, when I think about it I have to laugh). It took someone close to tell me to just be myself. From that day on preaching became an art. I began searching to find my own voice in order to draw upon it and make it meaningful, powerful, and heard. So through prayer and fasting, practice and failures, I found my voice.

I've had many great models of preachers, each with a unique voice that influenced my preaching: the Reverend P. Albert Williams of the African Methodist Episcopal Church; and the Reverends Tyrone D. Gordon, Lydia Waters, and Alfreda Wiggins of The United Methodist Church, to name a few. Each one was unique, but in each their love of God was exposed for all to see. Watching them, I wanted to do the same. As preachers we are sent to proclaim the living God to those who have not believed and to those who have not heard. It's a privilege, a divine gift, a gift of God's love.

Risk-Takers[*]
Matthew 25:14-30

In our passage, Jesus shares a parable about three servants that were entrusted with talents from their master. This is one of three parables shared with his disciples as his farewell sermon of caution, preparing them for a world of temptation and trouble. He alerts them through the parables to be ready and watchful for the Master's return. In the selected parable, three servants were entrusted with talents from their master; three servants, each given according to their ability. Although they were given a varying degree of responsibility, each was placed in the same position—delegated with the master's property. Each one was given something to work with. Each one was given a mission—take care of what belongs to me. But that's not all! Each one was given a choice of what to do with what they had. The master did not say, "You must go and apply in a certain manner." No...he gave it to them to do as they thought best. So two went out and put their money to work. They took a chance, expecting something in return. They went out with their minds made up that what their master had given them would come back twofold. They were risk-takers.

My question to you this evening is: "Are you a risk-taker?"

Risk-takers are movers and shakers. They are called by God to move. They are entrusted by God to shake things up. They do not dig; they don't hide; they move. If you recall, everything that God called forth into being moved. In fact, our God is a progressive God. Our God will move; our God will shake things up. Risk-takers are individuals that are not afraid of failure. Risk-takers understand that not everyone will be on your side. Risk-takers will walk alone. Numbers mean nothing to them. Their mind and their attention are deaf to distractions. They remain focused on their mission. Risk-takers believe all things are possible. They really believe "I can do all things through him [Christ] who strengthens me" (Philippians 4:13). Risk-takers expect the impossible. Risk-takers believe they can reach the unreachable...fight the unbeatable

[*] This sermon was preached February 20, 2011, at Bethel United Methodist Church, Peoria, Illinois, during 10:45 a.m. worship celebration as the church was moving toward expanding their church facility and ministries. View the preaching of this sermon on www.garrett.edu/styberg-bump/booker-jones

...move the unmovable...stand against the invincible. Risk-takers will take chances.

The Reverend Carlyle Stewart, in his book *The Empowerment Church*,[1] wrote that as followers of Jesus Christ our task is to make disciples. Unfortunately, many of our churches have taken on a different assignment. As people of God, we were created to glorify God. Unfortunately, many of our people have chosen to glorify things. And, because of their choices, we have churches that have become museums of the past or social clubs for the elite. Finance meetings become shouting matches; staff-parish committee meetings become pastor-bashing sessions; trustee meetings become mausoleum preservers; and evangelism, nurture, outreach, witness, and prayer ministers are missing in action.

The master returns. The one with five talents increased his five more. Let's see what he did. The one with the five talents:

- Started a new faith community.
- Brought in praise music.
- Made the main thing the main thing—Jesus Christ!
- Welcomed the stranger.
- Started a ministry of hospitality.
- Implemented new Bible study classes.
- Empowered people to be in ministry.
- Committed to evangelism.
- Opened the doors of the church.
- Empowered prayer warriors.
- Hired a minister of music.
- Started a new outreach ministry.

All that with five talents!

The one with two talents increased hers two more. Let's see what she did:

- Opened the doors to the hungry.
- Invited people different from herself to church.
- Started a volunteer ministry.
- Organized a prayer ministry.
- Introduced spiritual growth classes.

All with two talents!

Risk-takers are often misunderstood. People don't understand the drive within us that won't let us stop. We can't do anything different. Risk-takers are called aggressive, pushy, bossy, arrogant,

stubborn, demanding, and sometimes crazy—everything but a servant of God. Risk-takers have the "can't-help-its!" When the master places that talent in our hands we see possibilities. We can't
help it! We don't have time to process it. It's calling us! We don't
have time to ask permission or seek counsel. Our minds are already
fixed! The Master has entrusted this to us. At times we can't sleep
at night because there's a talent out there that we must put to work.
It needs to grow. We see increase! Risk-takers will take what they
have and give it, because they believe that if you "give, and it will
be given to you. A good measure, pressed down, shaken together,
running over, will be put into your lap" (Luke 6:38).

Churches that have risk-takers are churches that change. They
evolve. They grow. They take on the ways of Jesus. They're always
ready to do things in a new and innovative way. That's what Jesus
did. If you recall, Jesus did not always heal people with the same
method:
• He made mud to give sight to one man.
• He told another man to go, and as he went he was healed.
• One woman was healed by touching the hem of his garment.
• He told one man to come; his faith made him well.
• He told one man to go; his faith alone healed him.

Risk-taking churches will not always do things the same way.
The words, "We've always done it this way!" are not in the mission
statement.

Risk-takers don't always follow all the rules. Risk-takers will
work over forty hours a week. Risk-takers will miss their day off
occasionally. Risk-takers will invest their personal money on conferences and institutes. Risk-takers will often have to say they are
sorry for moving faster than the committees. And risk-takers will
refuse to move when they know God has a vision and purpose for
the church.

Risk-takers don't have time for foolishness. They understand
they have a vital assignment in building the church. They plant,
then watch as God gives the increase. They won't sit around talking about the preacher. They don't dip in other folks' business.
They put their talent to work! They don't lean back waiting to see
if someone else will do it. They don't try to take possession of what
doesn't belong to them. They know that "the earth is the LORD's,
and the fulness thereof... and they that dwell therein" (Psalm 24:1

KJV), and that it's "they that dwell therein" that we are called to serve. They understand that "they" means people! Risk-takers take a chance with people. The people are the talent that the Master has entrusted with us.

As risk-takers you take a chance on being ridiculed, mistreated, and talked about. But always remember, "*they*," the people, are God's creation. The people are God's property, and the Lord has entrusted them to you to do something with them. Therefore, you must love the people. You have heard it said before, "You can't lead the people if you don't love the people." Well, I must add, "You don't love the people if you're not willing to lead the people." Yes, church folk can be difficult. Yes, church folk can be hurtful. But you must learn how to protect yourself. If you recall, during the mid-year election, we saw commercials from politicians, each one challenging and opposing the other. If you've noticed, politicians surrounded themselves with people prepared to counteract any opposition that came up against them.

As leaders of God, opposition will come up against you. The enemy will attack. That's why we are instructed in the word of God to surround ourselves with the Holy Spirit. Dress in the full armor of God so that we can take a stand against the devil's schemes. For our struggle is not against flesh and blood but against the rulers, against the authorities, against the powers of this dark world, and against the spiritual forces of evil in the heavenly realms. But then you have the servant that goes out, digs a hole, and hides the master's property. He does nothing with what he has. The one talent that was given to him, he buries it and goes his merry way. He hinders any opportunity for growth. Don't be a hindrance!

The church's business is to summon people back to God. The church is called to help people live Spirit-filled lives and grow closer to God. The church is commissioned to make disciples for Jesus Christ. But there are people in the church who prevent anything from happening. They avoid the outreach program. They obstruct the worship celebration. They stop the Bible studies. They avoid the prayer ministries. There are those who try to stop anything that does not benefit them. If they can't lead it, then they ignore it.

The master came and the servant who hid his talent said, "Master...I knew that you are a hard man, harvesting where you have not sown and gathering where you have not scattered seed. So I was afraid and went out and hid your talent in the ground. See, here is what belongs to you" (Matthew 25:24-25 NIV). There are some people like this servant. They believe the accomplishments achieved just happened. They do not realize how much plowing that's needed; how much seed is scattered; how much sowing is required to have a harvest to gather. To them, it just happened. They don't understand how hard you work. They don't know how often you walked the floor, the hours at the church, and the tears you've shed. To them, it just happens! They don't know how many times you've thought about quitting. They don't know how many times you've questioned God and asked, "Why me?" To them, it just happens! So they hide the talent!

God does not have time for hiders. God is looking for risk-takers. Servants that will trust him even when it seems they cannot feel him; servants that will follow him even though it seems he's not present. God is looking for people that will honor him and not look to honor themselves. God desires servants who will take his talent and increase it. When the servant with five talents and the servant with two talents brought their increase, the master honored them. The master understood what they went through—*good and faithful*. The master knew the struggle—*good and faithful*. The master understood their hard work—*good and faithful*. The master respected their work—*good and faithful*.

There's a parable written by Sören Kierkegaard that tells about a community of ducks. One Sunday the ducks waddled off to their duck church to listen to their duck preacher. He quacked on and on about how their wings were gifts from God. Using these wings the ducks could go anywhere they desired and accomplish any task God gave them. Those wings could carry them into the presence of God himself. Shouts of "Amen" honked throughout the duck church. As the ducks left, they discussed what a wonderful message it was. And they all waddled back home, not realizing the gift within their wings.

You see, we serve a risk-taking God who has given us the ability to achieve any task that is brought before the church. We have wings; we have talents; we have a God who loves us, a Savior who saved us, the Holy Spirit that empowers us to do all things to the glory of God. Our God took a risk on us when he stepped down from his throne; God took a risk when he wrapped God's self in human flesh, was born of a virgin, called his name Jesus/Emmanuel—God with us!—laid in a manger. Jesus took a risk when he went to the synagogue and said (Luke 4:18-19 NIV), "The Spirit of the Lord is on me, because he has anointed me to preach good news to the poor." Risk-taking! "He has sent me to proclaim freedom for the prisoners." Risk-taking! "And recovery of sight for the blind." Risk-taking! "To release the oppressed." Risk-taking! "To proclaim the year of the Lord's favor." Risk-taking!

- Jesus healed the sick; gave sight to the blind; ate with sinners; saved the lost—he took a risk.
- The Pharisees and scribes tried to kill him; Judas betrayed him—but he took a risk.
- Peter denied; the other disciples were nowhere to be found—but he took a risk.

He walked up Calvary's Hill, laid on the cross, died for my sins, stepped down into the grave, but early Easter Sunday morning—he got up! Looked at you and me! He took a risk—with all power in his hands! Amen!

Note

1. Carlyle Stewart III, *The Empowerment Church: Speaking a New Language for Church Growth* (Nashville: Abingdon Press, 2001).

CHAPTER ELEVEN

A Transactional Relationship

Safiyah Fosua

When I began to preach, nearly thirty years ago, I approached preaching quite differently. I leaned more toward topical preaching and frequently, as young preachers do, selected a topic that interested me and then looked for texts that dealt with the topic—often stringing scores of unrelated texts together, along with far too many personal observations, into something that *I was certain* resembled a sermon. Over time, things have changed. Now I *start* with the text. Preaching holds the potential to help hearers realize that the human element is present in every part of the Bible—in the letters, in the historical passages, in the Levitical codes, in the Psalms, in the Prophets, in the Gospels—everywhere! Effective preaching transforms the *ancient* text into a *living* text with the hopes that it becomes a *lived* text in the lives of parishioners.

When I am not using the Revised Common Lectionary, texts for preaching come from my devotional reading of the Bible. My better sermons are often built around a text that will not let me go, one that I revisit again and again over a period of days or even months. When this happens, it feels like the passage is trying to say something important to me or to others, and I am drawn to it again and again until I hear—and share—the good news (or the words of warning) that the text brings. When I am preaching from the lectionary, I often read all the texts over and over, from different translations, aloud and silently, meditatively and exegetically, until I hear one of the passages speak louder than the others.

Most of my sermons are an eclectic blend of exposition and narrative. As needed, parts of the sermon are expository, with *preacher as narrator* bringing the congregation up to speed on helpful details about things like the *sitz im leben*, the geopolitical context, the use of language, or assumptions that the original audience may have had about relationships, taboos, norms, and deviances, so that later, the *denouement* of the sermon makes sense. Other parts of my sermons are in a storytelling style reminiscent of the old-time preacher, hoping to help the congregation see and feel and touch the very human elements of the story.

I am drawn to preach from Bible stories because they dramatize the human encounter with the divine—where divine intervention has taken place in some form, leaving us mortals to ponder *what does this mean?* I delight in scripture text that dramatizes the topsy-turvy nature of the gospel message where people who think they are on the upside of life are exposed in their poverty and those who are poor in spirit, physically ill, or deranged are restored to family and community to the glory of God. I believe this is the gist of the gospel message as forecasted both in Mary's Magnificat and in Jesus' inaugural sermon. No member of a congregation should be able to hear a sermon and remain unchanged. Similarly, no congregation should leave its community unchanged.

The preacher is the person who challenges, woos, and coaxes the congregation to embrace the lifestyle and ministry of Jesus Christ in ways that change their immediate surroundings and eventually their world! The greatest fodder for my sermons comes from the healing stories of the Bible from both Testaments. Those stories reveal a basic elemental need for God that is common to rich or poor, young or old, or people from any national or cultural background. The way most cultures regard the chronically ill or those who are debilitated is scandalous. The scandal of God's love for the poor, those who are sick, or those who are mentally unstable stands in direct contrast to our human tendencies and provides a way for us to see ourselves.

I have a love-hate relationship with pulpits. The pulpit is a powerful symbol—one often denied to some of our sisters in other denominations who are required to *teach from the floor*, when they should be preaching from the pulpit. But, for me the pulpit is more of an inconvenience because pulpits are designed for taller people and as such often become more barrier than symbol. For this reason, I often stand beside the pulpit or even preach in the midst of the people if it does not appear to make them uncomfortable. I almost always create a manuscript, but I preach from a skeletal outline. This is a discipline that I embraced in seminary. The manuscript serves as a place to test and perfect ways to get to my main point. Later, the skeletal outline is just a roadmap to keep me from chasing unproductive points. It bears mention that I consciously may choose not to follow this roadmap when I am on my feet in the unique transactional relationship between preacher and congregation and Holy Spirit.

I believe that preachers are charged to take their congregations on more frequent excursions into the otherness of God. We are to make sure that those who listen to our preaching with any frequency are confronted with a God who is greater than racism, than sexism, than poverty or politics. Through the foolishness of preaching we are able to see and taste the kingdom or reign of God enough to be dissatisfied with the status quo. I believe that our ancestors on this continent were able to prevail because of preaching that helped them focus on the majesty and sovereignty of God more than upon the myriad problems that they faced. God comes to lift the lowly, to level the mountainous pride of our age, and to lift up those whom the powerful have brought low. And if, perchance, the rich and powerful, who have often come to their wealth and position by less than honorable means, incline their ears and their hearts toward God, they too can be saved.

Walking Upright, Anyway!*
Luke 13:10-17

This is such an incredible story. On one hand, you have the visual image of a woman who has been bent over for an entire generation. Then, on the other, you have the image of mad-faced Pharisees, angry because the woman was healed on the wrong day of the week! I was so jarred by this passage several years ago that I wrote a letter to this woman, which I share with you today:

> I'm sure that no one understood your old point of view, Woman-Once-Bent-Over. Though some choose to look at the ground in despair and say, "I don't care"; for you, looking up was indeed difficult. How narrow your options had become over eighteen long years. Did you compare your prison with the prostitutes? They are in prison too. They, too, are captured by a *spirit* that holds them and forbids that they walk like the rest of us. Perhaps you compared your prison with the *workaholics* and the alcoholics who also are bound by things unseen. Or were you alone in your suffering, in your own private cell, left to contemplate how you would spend the rest of your life in that condition? What does it feel like, to finally be free from a prison that held you so long, Woman-Once-Bent-Over? Did you sigh with relief or rise in disbelief? How did it feel to stand once again? What were your thoughts? Did you prepare to run with glee? Surely all who had seen you before Jesus touched your life celebrated your good fortune. Or did they? More likely, you had to take time to come up with a story that would satisfy those who preferred seeing you bent over.[1]

The bent-over woman, unfortunately, dramatizes a scene played out far too often in our communities. Though the woman is hopelessly contorted and obviously in need of at least basic concern from us, her misery has become our wallpaper. Her misery has

---

* This sermon was preached at Warren United Methodist Church in Pittsburgh, Pennsylvania, on January 30, 2011. View the preaching of this sermon on www. garrett.edu/styberg-bump/fosua

become background noise for the six o'clock news. Her misery has become the condition that we look over so long, along with so many others, that we no longer see it—it and she are just part of the scenery that we avoid.

This poor woman had been down for so long, as the saying goes, that UP didn't cross *our* minds! We were so accustomed to seeing her bent over that it never occurred to us to help her stand up! The poor woman had endured eighteen years of looking down

>At gum on the floor
>>At dirty shoes
>>>At the nail polish on the stockings
>>>of a woman who is trying to convince the rest of us
>>>that she is all put together!

People on the underside of things often see all the places where we are unraveled.

If only we could know the agony behind the smile she smiles for our benefit:

"I have spent eighteen years of coming to the places where God is worshipped

>>>And making other folks comfortable
>>>with who I am.
>>>Of searching for *one good dress* at the
>>>Goodwill boutique
>>>To reduce the 'pity factor.'"

"I have spent eighteen years straining to look people in the eye
>Only to discover that it was not worth the effort
>>Because when I finally do manage to look up,
>>I can't help but notice that *they* are looking away,
>>>Pretending not to notice
>>>My deformity,
>>>My nonconformity,
>>>While secretly asking the question:
>>'What did she do to get paid back all this?'"

"I have endured eighteen years of people thinking I must be a sinner, of having my character in question. I have suffered through eighteen years of dealing with other folks' speculations about my soul."

Jesus broke the silence of her suffering: *A daughter of Abraham, whom Satan bound for eighteen long years.* Jesus' words were short-hand for "she did not bring this on herself!" This woman is a child of God.

How does Satan bind? How did Satan bind this woman? Was she bound by the inhuman actions of an insurance company that refused her treatment? Was she bound by the scarcity that comes from decades of failed economic policies? Was hers the long-term result of eating the wrong foods just to have *something* in the belly? Maybe she was bound by the broken promises of a broke-down boyfriend. Maybe it was the worry that comes from robbing Peter to pay Paul. Or that which comes when you know that the loan shark is about to get your late grandma's ring because you didn't get your money in time.

How does Satan bind you?

Jesus broke the silence. *When Jesus saw her, he called her over and said, "Woman, you are set free from your ailment."*

He called her over,

Just as he had gone out of his way to talk to a Samaritan woman at Jacob's well.

Just as he had gone out of his way to talk to an invalid at the pool of Bethesda.

He called her over; he went out of his way to engage her.

Just as he had done at a funeral procession in Nain.

He called her over and engaged her—she who had spent a generation looking at shoes, and dirt, and things that people threw on the ground.

He engaged the *squeegee man* in conversation.

He talked to the woman with the shopping cart full of plastic.

He had a serious conversation with the man who has too many visible tattoos for our liking.

He was kind to the teenager who looks like her clothes got shrunk in the dryer!

He engaged the elderly woman living on a fixed income whose coat is full of holes; or the old man whose suit smells.

Jesus engaged the person we spend too little time with. Jesus *called her over*, spoke to her, and laid his hands on her.

He laid his hands on her,

Hands, plural
> Both hands

Not one finger

Not three fingers
> Both hands

Healing hands

Healing words.

SHE WAS HEALED!

Immediately she stood up straight and began praising God.

SHE GOT UP PRAISING GOD!

Then *they* sat down with their arms crossed raising the devil!

Six days! Said the leader of the synagogue,

There are six days on which work ought to be done; come on those days and be cured, and not on the Sabbath day. Six days!

We set one day aside for rest, not work. Jesus, you did it wrong. You did not follow the rules. We don't like it!

(What was it they didn't like: Jesus working on the Sabbath or the possibility that the squeegee man might join their church?)

Six days!

The words were a smoke screen for *but I was comfortable with her misery.* He didn't even direct his words to Jesus; he spoke to the crowds with a tone that said: "Don't think any of the rest of you is going to get healed up in here!"

Not on the Sabbath! We've got a program!

Besides, it is work to get *you* healed any day—you certainly shouldn't be healed on the Sabbath!

You hypocrites! Again, Jesus broke the silence.

You hypocrites! Does not each of you on the Sabbath untie his ox or his donkey from the manger, and lead it away to give it water?

If Jesus were responding today, how might he say this? You hypocrites! You are kinder to your lap dog than you are to people! You have doggie parks while there are children with no parks at all. And some dogs receive better healthcare than the working poor. You hypocrites!

When he said this, all his opponents were put to shame.

At a recent Festival of Homiletics in Minneapolis, Minnesota, Barbara Lundblad, professor of homiletics at Union Theological Seminary, confronted a sea of pastors with the lack of shame displayed during the 2008 presidential elections. She chided that the church needs to learn to blush again and that the church needs to learn to stand up for what it believes to be right again. What does it take to put us to shame?

Does it take Addie Polk? Addie Polk is a ninety-year-old who attempted suicide while being evicted from her home during the mortgage crisis. Does it take a hurricane, like Katrina, or a flood? What does it take to put us to shame?

It is a shame that some families are being forced to choose between gasoline and food!

It is a shame that we have so many children who are hungry and have no healthcare!

It is a shame that we have completely lost our moral standing as a nation!

It is a shame that we have gone from protecting one another to killing one another in the night!

It is a shame that we have gone from helping one another to competing against one another!

But it is a *greater shame,* my brothers and my sisters in the ministry, that so many of us sat by and watched all this happen because we were too busy with the building fund or the pastor's anniversary!

Look at Jesus. What did he do with the woman bent over, bound by Satan for a generation?

He ignored protocol.
He ignored dividing lines.
He ignored classism.
He ignored gender politics.
He ignored ageism.
    He called her over—
    He engaged this woman.
    He put his hands on her—she was not untouchable.
    He healed her.
    And then, he defended her right to be whole!

So far, we have been dealing with us and them; insiders and out-siders; people bent over and people standing by watching their misery. But what if the one bent over is *you*?

There are too many days that I feel bent over. There are too many days that I feel like Satan has tried to bind me, when folks work entirely too hard to remind me:

That I am a woman.
  That I am a Black woman.
    That I am a Black woman born in the early fifties.
      That I am a Black woman born in the early fifties called to preach!

That I serve in a denomination that is 90 percent White in a coun-try that is more than one-third non-White!

Sometimes I feel like that bent-over woman—even in the com-pany of Christians. The *rules* we enact—rules that attempt to describe who is acceptable and who is not, who can come to church and who cannot, who can serve and which hoops they have to jump through. But I am encouraged, because in spite of all that we Christians do to frustrate the grace of God, that woman *still got healed in church*!

Sisters and brothers, Jesus is calling us today with outstretched hands. It is time for us to break free from the things that bind us:

Things that keep us immobilized,
Things that keep us bent over and pitiful.
It is time for us to rise up and praise God with our actions, with purposeful responses to the challenges that face our communi-ties both inside and outside of the church house. It is time for the church for which Christ died
To stand up!
  To praise God!
    To defy the critics!
      To follow Jesus in engaging those who often get swept to the side!
To erase the social boundaries and classism that are threatening to sap our very life's blood.

It is time for us to stand up, in spite of what the resident Pharisees say, and in spite of what the street committee says. It is time for us to follow Jesus in healing people *and* defending their right to be whole. We are sons and daughters of Abraham. God never intended for us to walk through life bent over. We are sons and daughters of the Most High God. God never intended for us to be bound.

It does not matter what happens on Wall Street or Main Street—in the White House or in *your* house! It does not matter what comes up, or what goes down! We are people of God, and God's hands are upon us, making it possible for us to *walk upright*—anyway!

Note

1. "Walking Upright, Anyway" from *Mother Wit: 365 Meditations for African American Women*, by Safiyah Fosua (© Safiyah Fosua).

CHAPTER TWELVE

An Intimate Discourse on the Holy

Dorothy Watson-Tatem

Preaching is an intimate discourse with people about that which is holy. Anything sacred is intimate beyond our imagining. Preaching is the foolishness of mere human beings attempting to fathom and explain the divine nature and dynamics of the Godhead. The particularity of time and place is most human; and God, who is beyond this confinement, pours out the divine self in this narrow scope that the divine might be known to humankind. Pain and suffering have brought me to a commitment and intimacy with God through Christ by the power of the Holy Spirit that keeps the preaching event from being just an intellectual exercise or a showcase of my gifts or even a desire to be in competition with others who savor the preaching event.

Preaching as divine foolishness utilizes the inadequacy of human thinking, analysis, delivery, and the human person to proclaim the reality of God. To preach under one's own power is akin to being moved by the photographs taken by the Hubble telescope and found in a coffee table book. However, to preach under the anointing of the Holy Spirit is, minimally, like viewing the heavens through the actual telescope or, maximally, to be jettisoned into space to experience the universe firsthand. Even so, our humanity precludes our seeing the whole.

Deliverance, acceptance, and triumph all inform the sermonic moments and breathe integrity into the challenges, aspirations, and victories of those who receive the sermon.

Pain and suffering have given me patience, and this quality is precious in doing exegesis. The preacher must give diligent attention to the integrity of the text, probe beneath the surface meaning of the pericope, and then make the findings comprehensible to the hearers. To do such requires daily attention to the sermon and to its impact upon the preacher prior to delivery, and it requires an openness to revision even in the midst of the event of proclamation. Have you ever encountered two sermons that are the same, even though the particular time and place in which they were preached, and the preachers who proclaimed them, have no connection to each other? Our confinement or physical restriction does not at all confine God. On the other hand, God customizes the message for the people in the particular time and place in order that their needs are addressed and they are informed again that God is with them.

Whether the sermon gives praise or joy, convicts or warns, encourages, instructs, or condemns, the good news is to be proclaimed, that God is with the individual and the corporate body. The hearers need to be informed continually that nothing can separate them from the love of God in Christ Jesus! The good news is that heaven and earth may pass away, but God made humankind as eternal beings who have the option to be always with God. The kingdom of God begins now, not later! This is the good news that the community of faith must hear and share repeatedly!

The occasion may direct me to find its reflection in scripture; I may meditate on the lectionary readings and note the ones that arrest my mind and heart; I may jot down possibilities for future sermons that are triggered by circumstances; and then there are those times when a Spirit prompt gives me the text. But regardless of the process I use to select scripture for preaching, it must be undergirded by a sense that God has made known the text. Through it all I simply want to get beneath the surface of the passage to the wonder, the soul-wrenching and the transformation, the God-encounter!

I prefer to preach from the floor rather than behind a lofty pulpit because I want to engage the hearers through eye contact, vocal tonality, even body language that underscores the message (but does not become an obstacle to the content of the sermon). Excitement and passion about the text are the greatest influences on my sermon because the message is like a force in my being that must be released. A love for drama influences the order of the sermon, the physical movement, and an acute attention to the reception of the hearers, which may demand revision in the midst of the preaching event. The hearers' understanding (not necessarily their agreement) is meant to accomplish a different perception of the divine, an engagement with the divine, and a response to the divine.

The late Elder Pauline Crawford was an early influence on my preaching. She was insistent that there was nothing more powerful than the wedding of the human intellect and the Holy Spirit. The late Bishop William Pugh, whose formal education was not beyond elementary school, used the *sitz im leben* more powerfully than any preacher I have ever heard in order to ground the sermon and then apply the text to life. Both of these preachers were members of Mt. Sinai Holy Churches of America, in which I grew up. Dr. Gennifer Brooks, Dr. James Forbes, Dr. Renita J. Weems, the Reverend Angelin Jones Simmons, Dr. Fred Craddock, the Reverend Kirbyjon Caldwell, Dr. Gardner Taylor, and others bring the biblical narrative to the door of our souls through their intellect and concern for the quality of life and what we are called by God to do about it. They preach with the inspiration of the Holy Spirit so that conviction remains a viable force that calls one to a decision about self, others, service beyond the church, and relationship to God. One does not sit passively under such preachers!

As a preacher I am most intrigued with the audience. Who is there and what is it that they need from the word of God? I do not know specifically; however, I believe passionately that because of the preparations, prayer, exegetical work, conversations, attention to the events of the times, and some internal scrutiny, that which will come forth in the delivery will be the beginning, the continuation, or the definitive declaration in someone's conversation with God.

Vitis Vinea Feder or Jesus Wept; What About Us?*
John 15:1-8

The disciples were about to experience the devastation of their lives. They had already seen and participated in the glory of the entry into Jerusalem, but they were about to be devastated, blindsided. Knowing this, Jesus was about to have a talk with them so that they would somehow in retrospect recall the words of Jesus and not be destroyed by what was to come. So Jesus says to them, I am the true vine, or I am the *real* vine. Now the disciples resonated with this because they had heard this vine metaphor before.

Israel was to be the vine, but she messed up. Isaiah came through and said, "Israel, you were to be the vine, but you have become sour grapes." They did not get it then, so Jeremiah also said, "You are rotten and you are worthless grapes." And if that wasn't enough, Ezekiel composed a song and said, "You were once a lush and wonderful vine, but you have failed and now you are nothing but some vine, some shriveled-up something in the desert, never to be green again." Israel as the vine was God's plan B. Now Jesus comes and says, "I am the true vine. I am it." The disciples knew that they were feeling good because a new dispensation was coming in, and when Jesus said "I am the vine" they could see themselves wrapped up in that.

What is this vine? What is Jesus talking about? I am not talking about the kudzu vine. If you live in the South you know about the kudzu vine. They brought it from Japan. It looked nice and in an impatient society it caught on because it grew quickly, and if you wanted it quickly you bought kudzu. It could not be contained. It grew and it grew. So now they work at containing kudzu.

Another vine is poison ivy. It shows up sometimes in hidden places. You're just walking along on a path that is gorgeous and you brush along something and it's okay. Then after a while the epidermis starts to erupt, and it starts to get a little red. Then you have to get some calamine and some cortisone to stop the itching. Poison ivy is not the vine.

---

* This sermon was preached at the 2003 Convocation for Pastors of Black Churches held in Houston, Texas. View the preaching of this sermon on www.garrett.edu/styberg-bump/watson-tatem

But there is ivy, pretty stuff. For those with lawns, you just plant the ivy and it will just cover, and you don't have to worry about mowing the grass. It can grow up the side of a building or over the ground or whatever. It's nice, but it's just ground cover or wall cover. It ain't the vine. All of these follow the shape of the place they are in. If the place has little hills, then they wind and bend over little hills. If the place is elevated, then they elevate because of terrain; but they aren't the vine.

Then there is *Vitis Vinea Feder;* that's grapes, y'all. It's a fruit vine, and fruit vines have to be vertical so that when they are up then the bees can do some cross-pollination. When they are up, they are closer to the sun. When they are up, they don't get trampled on. Fruit vines don't just give up pretty leaves like ivy. Fruit vines don't give up pretty flowers. Fruit vines got to give up some fruit. So Jesus said, "I am the vine." I'm vertical. "I'm the vine." Then, because he was talking to folk who don't know, he said God is the caretaker of the vine. God owns the vine, and God alone does the cutting. God alone decides what needs cutting.

Sometimes this scripture is carelessly preached and folk act like there is the world and there is the vine, like this is what this pericope is talking about. No, it ain't. It is talking about the church. It is about the church. Jesus is the vine and kudzu ain't coming out of that vine. The branch that comes out of the vine has got the DNA of the vine. It is part and parcel of the vine. The vine begets the branch; that is why God, who owns the vine, decides who gets cut off. This isn't about the world. God decides who gets pruned.

When you read the passage it says, "You have been cleansed by the word that you have heard" (John 15:3, paraphrased). The Greek meaning for cleansed is the same as pruned. So we can paraphrase that and say the Word is the cutting tool, and scripture says of the Word that the Word cuts where the soul and the spirit meet. The Word cuts where the joint and the marrow come together.

There are criteria that God uses for cutting. When God sees a branch that is dried up, God starts cutting. God starts cutting until there is the point where the juice of the vine begins to come forward. When you cut a vine and you get to the live part, there is some weeping that happens; but you don't tell God which branch to cut. There was something in scripture about wheat and tares, but it didn't tell us to do the division. It said God makes the decision when it comes to those branches we forget, but God cuts until there is weeping.

Then there is some pruning. The whole of the vine is subject to cutting, not just the good or the bad. We get that mixed up. "Oh, the bad folks get cut off." Oh, no! Everybody gets cut. It is the depth of the cutting—the depth of the cutting!—that makes the difference of whether you are still on the vine or cut off. So, for those who possess the fruit of the Spirit, you love other folk, you have an exuberance about life, you have some serenity and a willingness to stick with things and folk. The fruit of the vine is a sense of compassion in the heart and a conviction in holiness. You've got fruit when you are loyal to commitment. You've got fruit when you don't need to have your way. You've got fruit when you get disciples. But even when you are a fruitful branch, you have to be cut too.

I talked to a winery in California and said, "Tell me about this cutting stuff." They said, "Well, we prune." I said what you pruning for? They said, "We can get more fruit because the nutrients, the essence has a shorter way to go. They are concentrated, so they get all up in the short form of the branch and we get more bundles of *Vitis Vinea Feder*. But it hurts." How do you know it hurts? "Because when you prune back, the vine starts to weep, because you don't have to go through dead stuff. You are going through some live stuff." So the vine, as soon as you begin to cut, that good vine begins to weep. The owner has a plan. The owner wants much fruit, and the owner says, "Got to cut back the branch a little." That is not all. The winery owner said to me, "Not only do we prune or cut back but when the grapes, the bundles, begin to form, we go to the bunch and we start pinching off grapes from the bunch." Why are you doing that? Why are you pinching back the fruit? "Because we want big fruit, and if we pinch off some of the grapes from the bundle then those nutrients begin to go into the branches of the bunch and because not all of the grapes are on the bunch then those that remain begin to expand. They begin to get bigger, and so we pinch back so we can get some bigger fruit."

But the vine is still going to weep a little bit when you pinch back. Jesus wept. In John 11, it says that the folk were crying because Lazarus had died. They were weeping because Jesus had let him die. Mary and Martha said, "If you had been here, Jesus,

108

this would not have happened." And so Mary cried and so Jesus looked at her and then Martha cried. Then the moaners, they cried. Jesus looked and some folk tell me that they did not understand that the life and resurrection was there and was not dependent upon time, and Jesus wept. They did not get it. Boy, he really loves Lazarus. But don't you weep, pastors, when you have worked and done all you can and the folk just don't get it. They see you looking sad, and they think you have an attitude, and they say, "He or she is disturbed?" because of events they can't understand and what you are disturbed about is that the folks don't get it. Jesus wept.

Jesus wept again. He entered Jerusalem. He was the man, the King, the Ruler; and he looked out over the Holy City. And he said that God had sent the prophets that you might be the first partakers of the blessing of God; you, Jerusalem, are to shine out and let the world know that God is God and there is no other power besides God. But you rejected him, and Jesus wept again. But he isn't finished weeping.

Another time Jesus wept, as Dr. Simmons said, Jesus had a bad day, and that bad day got Jesus jailed. The bad time got Jesus jailed and persecuted, and they strung him up on that wooden cross. They took the vine, but it was vertical. They took the vine and strung him up on a piece of wood, and while he was there he did all sorts of good things. But suffering is suffering, and after a while suffering begins to get to you, and Jesus could not take it, it seemed, anymore. While he was vertically strung up and horizontally stretched out, he said, *"Eli, Eli, lema sabachthani?"* *"Eli Eli,"* a personal intimate name, *Eli*. "My God, my God, why have you forsaken me?" But he did not have the right to come down off the cross. He had the power and everything he needed to step down off the cross, but he stayed there despite the fact that he could not find his God. He stayed in spite of the fact that his God was not reaching out to him. Understand that Jesus wept and they took him out.

Let me tell you, when humans think they take God out, let me tell you, they only work into God's plan. So they supposedly took your Jesus. They took the vine out. They did not cut the branch. They said, "We're going to take the vine, and if we take the vine, we've got the branches." So they thought they would cut the vine, the vine looked dead, the vine looked like it had no life. Then they took the vine and put the vine in a dark place, a place for the dead. They put the vine in a hidden place. They said, "We've taken the vine out, now we have got the victory." Here comes one day, they still got the victory. The second day, they got the victory; but on the next day, they said, "Excuse me."

It's all right to cry, it is normal to feel forsaken, and when you go back home you are going to find that someone, if you are dead, just cut you off. That's God. But for 99.9 percent of you, you are going to go home and find that God has been pruning your fruit. Things that you thought were fine, are cut back. The general church is going through a cutback. But God is the caretaker. God wants a church that the gates of hell will not prevail against.

Pastor, there will be a ministry that you had in place that you thought was bearing fruit. Bishops, you are going to have some initiatives that you knew were sound and they were okay. District Superintendents, there were things that you left in place, and you saw the fruit before you left. Pastors, those ministries that you have that you could even see souls coming in, there is going to be a pinch back that happened while you were gone.

This is what is going to happen. You can weep, and that is all right. You can cry out, "My God, why have you forsaken me?" and that's all right; but what you have got to do is just stay on that vine 'cause resurrection is coming. You got to stay on that vine because God wants some more fruit. Stay on the vine because God wants bigger fruit. It isn't your fruit. It isn't your vine, and you ain't even your own branches. You belong to God. God said in John 15:16, "You did not choose me but I chose you. And I appointed you." He says, "I am the owner and caretaker of the vine. I chose you and then I appointed you. You don't know what your purpose is: go and bear fruit." We're not talking about wild grapes. We are talking about fruit that will last. God wants Zinfandel. God wants Pinot. God wants Chamberlain. Then God said in the word that "I, God, will give you whatever you ask in my name." So when it looks like the vine is dead, it isn't. It's you. When it looks like your fruit is shot to pieces, it isn't. God is pruning. When it looks like your ministry is so little, it isn't. God is going to pinch back. "I am giving you this command so you will love one another" (John 15:17, paraphrased). You won't be so stressed out worrying about your fruit that you can't love somebody. Mad folk can't love anybody. Sad folk can't love anybody. Despondent folk can't love anybody. But it is a joy. It's a joy. Why are you crying and laughing at the same time? 'Cause I know God is up to something. I know God is up to something, 'cause my fruit is going to grow.

This is the word of the Lord to you here today. God wanted me to focus on that cutting and the bleeding. When God prunes us, the vine weeps. We don't want Jesus to weep because we have been cut off. We want Jesus to weep because we hurt for the moment. Joy is coming. Weeping is part of being on the vine. But just for a little while and in a few hours, here comes joy. You will see it like a glimmer on the horizon, and then it begins to mushroom and to bloom, because joy comes in the morning.

Our Lord wept, and we will too.

But he got up. He got up, and so will we.

CHAPTER THIRTEEN

Continuing the Work of Christ

Robert O. Simpson

My theology of preaching recognizes that preaching is the very act of proclaiming the gospel, and it becomes an instrument of God's saving word. Preaching is a redemptive deed. A sermon, the substance of preaching, is not a lecture; an essay; a theological dissertation; a discussion of social, political, and world affairs; or instruction in morals, but God's saving approach to the souls of men and women. And I operate from the position that preachers are partners with God in God's continuing redemptive activity. When I began the pastoral enterprise, I believed that preaching was the way the pastor/preacher got his "agenda" across to his hearers. I quickly learned that it is *not* my "agenda" that needs to be pressed; instead, my purpose is to use sermons as a way to make folk "God-conscious"—to influence and aid people to live religiously.

Human beings do not live in a vacuum. Their lives are influenced by everyday issues, situations, and circumstances. The preacher and the sermon must meet people where they are and try to minister to their life situations. The preacher must take the time to engage the lives of the people through the word of God revealed in scripture, in the lives of the people, in society, and in the pastor's own life. Preaching requires this multidimensional engagement of preacher and people, but with God as the center or focal point of that engagement. The apostle Paul told the Corinthians that he and his associates were "ambassadors for Christ, since God is making his appeal through us" (2 Corinthians 5:20a). Paul's message was that their preaching was a continuation of the work of Christ. Our preaching must confirm that we, too, are ambassadors for Christ using the gospel as an instrument of God's saving love. The good news of the gospel, God's redemption of sinful humanity, is still the most important message for humanity.

In selecting a text for preaching, I am guided in part by my own devotional life. The time I spend daily with God involves reading the Scriptures and other devotional material as well as prayer and meditation. One of the resources that I use as I engage in my ritual of morning devotion is the *Upper Room Disciplines*. This may occasionally focus my attention on a text or I might select a text dealing with a liturgical season, such as Advent, Christmas, or Epiphany. The most important criterion for selecting a text for preaching is the message that I believe God wants me to deliver to the people. I usually allow the text to speak to me and see how that text might, in turn, speak to the waiting congregation.

Preparing a sermon takes time. The development of the sermon takes its shape from the perceived need and the particular message it seeks to deliver. Sermon type or style is of little or no importance; for me, those considerations are subject to the contents of the sermon and the offering of God's redemptive love that it provides. Not for me the facility of selecting a text, doing the interpretation, and developing the sermon in the space of a few days. I usually identify two or three texts and begin working on them over the course of two or three weeks. In doing so, I am able to follow through with a particular message or focus with sufficient repetition that the hearers have multiple opportunities to receive the message. This does not mean necessarily that I preach only sermon series, but I find that giving attention to several texts at the same time aids my process of exegesis and biblical interpretation. Additionally, since the situations in society are reflected over significant time periods, this provides an opportunity for greater reflection between the biblical and the current context.

Many times, I use, by way of introduction, some current event, societal challenge, or life situation to introduce the topic or focus of the sermon. But this is done with an eye toward the impact these entities have on the salvation of men and women. At some point in every sermon, the preacher must ask "what God would have us do" with racism, classism, sexism, our assault on the planet earth, or any of the many and varied ways that we allow sin to deny the peace and justice that is the realm of God. What is the Christian's challenge to all of them? It is the task of the preacher to address these issues and help the congregation experience the grace of God that alone can overcome the forces of sin and evil.

Preparing to speak to the issues of human life and engaging the congregation in the dialog of the sermon necessitates great care. In order to ensure that the words of the sermon fit the intent that created it, I normally use an outline to help organize my thoughts for presentation and to diminish the chances of repetition. I find that preaching from the pulpit also helps me maintain that focus, and while I am committed to the message and deliver it with the intensity it requires, I find that having the congregation sing a hymn immediately before and after the sermon helps focus and then reinforce the message of the sermon.

There are three specific preachers who have influenced my preaching. First is my maternal grandfather, William O. Carrington, who was an A.M.E. Zion Church pastor for sixty-plus years. Second is Gardner C. Taylor, the acknowledged Dean of American Preachers. Third is Ernest T. Campbell, the late pastor of the Riverside Church in New York City. In my estimation, these stalwarts of proclamation have influenced the lives of many people. As I try to follow in their footsteps, my prayer is that the words that I preach will also influence the lives of my hearers as they try to live religiously, and my hope is that I can meet that preaching challenge always.

Make Your Dungeons Shake*
Acts 16:25-34

Our lesson for today is one of the most powerful and moving in all of the Scriptures. It is the story of Paul and Silas and their encounter with a slave girl and its aftermath. By way of background, Paul and Silas were on their way to a "place of prayer," notably a synagogue, when they happened upon a young slave girl who had a spirit of divination. In other words, she was mad; crazy; full of the Devil. Yet in her madness she exhibited the ability to give oracles to guide men about the future, like a soothsayer. She had fallen into the hands of some unscrupulous men who used her misfortune for their personal gain. There are always those around who may want to exploit you and your situation.

At their meeting, Paul became vexed at her shouting and otherwise acting-out—so much so that he turned and commanded the evil spirit to come out of her. That cured her madness but caused fury to rage in her handlers. These handlers began to plot against Paul and Silas for ruining their revenue stream. They succeeded, and Paul and Silas were arrested. At their arrest, the magistrate not only jailed them but had them put in the "innermost cell and fastened their feet in the stocks" (Acts 16:24). The innermost part of the prison sounds like a dungeon to me.

These men of God, followers of Jesus Christ, are in a dungeon, a place of little or no light, dark. A place that was dank, to say the least. A place that no doubt was damp and with an odor. An unfinished space with a dirt floor and rough-hewn walls. Possibly a place that was vermin-infested. A place of isolation and confinement. A dead end.

The tragic thing was that Paul and Silas were arrested, imprisoned, and maltreated for doing good—for freeing this young slave girl of her madness and from being used and abused. It is characteristic of men that if their pockets are threatened they get up in arms and retaliate. These men's livelihood had been threatened and undermined by the goodness of Paul.

---

* This sermon was preached on November 21, 2010, Christ the King Sunday at Janes United Methodist Church in Brooklyn, New York, on the occasion of the church's 151st anniversary. View the preaching of this sermon on www.garrett.edu/styberg-bump/simpson

Thankfully, Paul and Silas were religious men who believed in a power greater than their own. So rather than become discouraged or dismayed or distracted, rather than pity themselves and their situation, at midnight they began to pray and sing hymns to God. Midnight—that darkest of hours. Midnight—when all is still and silent. Midnight—when most folk are asleep. Midnight—when maladies hurt worse than they do in the daytime. At midnight Paul and Silas began to pray and sing hymns to God. Their approach to God at that midnight hour was no doubt humbling, with penitence and even a touch of thanksgiving that their situation was not any worse than it was. The hymns they sang were from the Psalter because there was no *United Methodist Hymnal,* no *Baptist Standard Hymnal,* no *Songs of Zion,* no *Gospel Pearls,* no Sankey. The only songs they could sing were psalms. So in the dungeon at midnight they perhaps sang Psalm 27, "The Lord is my light and my salvation."

Those of us who have been in dungeons might join them in adapting Psalm 27 to be sung:

The Lord is my light and my salvation,
the Lord is my light and my salvation,
the Lord is my light and my salvation.
Whom shall I fear?

In the time of trouble he shall hide me,
in the time of trouble he shall hide me,
in the time of trouble he shall hide me.
Whom shall I fear?

Wait on the Lord and be of good courage,
wait on the Lord and be of good courage,
wait on the Lord and be of good courage.
He will strengthen thine heart.

Whom shall I fear? Whom shall I fear?
The Lord is the strength of my life.
Whom shall I fear?

And bless God, at their praying and singing, the ground began to shake. So much so that the foundations of the prison were shaken and the doors opened and everyone's fetters came off.

This is a powerful story and one that needs to be retold and understood in our day because some of us are in dungeons today. Some of us are living in dark places—places that are spiritually dark—because we do not know the light of Christ. Dungeons where sin, in its many forms, is ever-present.

Some of us are in dungeons of despair because we can't see any way out of our debt or sickness or loveless relationships or depression.

Some of us are facing what we believe for us will be our dead end. There is nothing worse than being in the dungeon of hopelessness.

But, thank God, this story of Paul and Silas doesn't end in the dungeon. When you believe in God, there is always a way out. Always a way around. Always a tunnel through. Always a light for your exit. Always a way when there seems to be no way.

How can we make our dungeons shake?

When faced with life's dungeons, we too must learn to pray and sing hymns to God. For in the dungeon, God can pray you through. Some of us don't pray unless or until we're in trouble, and then we cry, "O Lord, have mercy." In this life, we can ill afford not to stay "prayed-up" and with a song of hope on our lips.

In the dungeon, God's power is manifest in our weakness. Amid the isolation and confinement of some dungeon experience, we realize that God is able. Able to be and do anything and everything we need.

In the dungeon we can reconnect with the author and finisher of our faith. In the dungeon, when all seems against you, you can look around and find a way. In the dungeon, if you pray right, you can trust God and never doubt his providence. In the dungeon, if you hold to God's unchanging hand, the very foundations of your troubles and woes will begin to shake and doors will be opened and your fetters will come off.

Some folk finally find God in the dungeon. Some folk let their egos go in the dungeon. Some folk finally let their burdens down in the dungeon.

When that day finally comes, you'll be able to testify, *"Free at last! Free at last! Thank God Almighty, I'm free at last!"*

CHAPTER FOURTEEN

A Timely and Relevant Word

James E. Swanson, Sr.

All preaching for me is an exercise in seeking to give God-breathed answers to the problems that perplex humanity. Those answers may come from the reading of the scriptural foundation for the sermon or from lessons learned in life. Preaching allows me the opportunity to serve God by being a conduit of God's word that hopefully blesses people as I discern the movement of God through prayer and reflection, seeking to find answers given by others that I trust, as I study and meditate on the biblical text or the truth I see and encounter in life. Preaching is at its best when the preacher experiences not only the word but also the people and the set of circumstances that gives shape and form to that particular body of people to whom the proclamation is addressed. It is the preacher's responsibility to hold in tension what the text says and what the current reality is for the hearers of the sermon.

Early in my preaching journey I relied heavily on the opinions and writings of others. It has been a journey in which I have grown to trust not just authors who think like me but some who challenge me in their interpretation of the text. I am more open to receiving information not only from biblical scholars but from others who model biblical principles or express ideas that come through their experiences and training. In addition, in preaching, I am more and more willing to share my personal testimony of God's interaction in my life and life lessons I have learned.

I am also guided by the issues and challenges facing the people I am serving. There are times that I perceive the Holy Spirit challenging me to address a particular issue, and I will search the scripture to see if there is a text that helps underpin the idea that the Holy Spirit is seeking to birth. There is one scripture that I hold on to when I am preparing the sermon. "The thief comes only to steal and kill and destroy; I have come that they may have life, and have it to the full" (John 10:10 NIV). I hear this guiding me in the back of my mind and underneath all of my thought processes. How can the Holy Spirit aid me in helping build people and usher them into a relationship with Christ, others, and themselves that will lead them to their ultimate good?

Whether I choose to use an expository style in order to unpack a central theological point; or seek to give the listeners a more in-depth understanding of the biblical text and its relevance for their lives; or go more into detail about the meaning and implication of an issue or concern, I try to understand or sense what the Holy Spirit is asking or demanding that I address in my sermon. I believe preaching needs to be timely and relevant. For that purpose I seek to spend some time in prayer, during which I am doing more listening than talking to God. I also try to take some time to listen to the people to whom I am preparing to preach. This is more a reading of the environment, circumstances, and conditions in which my listeners find themselves residing.

Depending on the amount of preparation time available, I will live with the text for some time before beginning to write the sermon. I read what others have to say about the text and what my heart is saying. The idea that emerges becomes the heart and soul of the sermon. It is the problem I'm seeking to address. Determining how to illustrate the problem so that people can not only hear it but see it involves looking for illustrations that help clarify and illuminate the problem as one that demands the people's attention. Flushing out answers that I believe are embedded in the text also requires looking for illustrations that make the answers clearer, that help me preach the message. In the end, the answer comes by laying everything before the Holy Spirit.

As an African American born, raised, and educated in the United States of America, it would be very difficult for me to be effective in preaching and ignore those areas of peace and justice that are crying out to be heard and taken seriously in my community. How I interpret the biblical text is so heavily influenced by the culture that produced me and the experiences that have shaped me that I cannot help but speak to the heartbeat of my people who long for justice. I live in a world torn by violence, and I must speak to this as contrary to God's expressed will for humanity.

A preacher is called to prophesy, to speak forth from God to contemporary issues. That is the most challenging part of my preaching when as a bishop I must do so in the various cultures that are part of The United Methodist Church. It was the position of my teacher, the Reverend Edwards Isaac Clark, and now mine, that you are at your best when you can develop into your true preaching self. I realize that for some time as a person develops his or her style of preaching, that person will emulate others. I guess I wanted to be a combination of Harry V. Richardson and C. L. Franklin; but when I discovered I couldn't sing, the C. L. desire left; and when I discovered I couldn't be still, the Harry V. went too. I don't know what you call my delivery style. Some people call me a whooper, but I am a very emotional person and therefore my emotions are evident in my preaching. I am also one who is at ease with allowing others to know me so that transparency is a part of my style of delivery. One of the preachers who influenced my development is the Reverend Arthur J. Bondage, my first pastor. He was very simple and spoke to a child's heart. It is my hope that in the simple act of my preaching, people will encounter the Holy Spirit speaking to them and their concerns.

The Church at Its Best[*]
Ephesians 4:1-16

The gifts he gave were that some would be apostles, some prophets, some evangelists, some pastors and teachers, to equip the saints for the work of ministry, for building up the body of Christ, until all of us come to the unity of the faith and of the knowledge of the Son of God, to maturity, to the measure of the full stature of Christ. (Ephesians 4:11-13)

To the measure of the full stature of Christ! I declare to you tonight that the world needs the church to be at its best. The world needs the church to be at its best.

The title of the sermon comes to us from the writings of a man who wrote a book entitled *The Church at Its Best*. Bernard happened to be traveling in Tampa, Florida. And while he was traveling he happened to notice on the marquee of the church this sign: "The world at its worst needs the church to be at its best." The world at its worst needs the church to be at its best.

I don't know about you, but it only takes a kind of casual viewing of the television or casual reading of newspaper today to see that in many quarters of this world we see things that we could in many ways characterize as the world at its worst, things that appall us. Some of us might have thought those things might have been over, only to wake up from our sleep and find out that there have been those doing what we used to say back home in Houston, that's waiting in the cuts. Biding their time and waiting for the opportune moment to show their true colors. You see, you can only be politically correct for so long. You can only act as if you love who you don't love for so long. You all remember the movie about Roscoe Jenkins? As his cousin approaches, Roscoe tells his fiancée, "Hide your purse," and as his cousin tries to embrace him Roscoe does the old slow drag dance. And then when his cousin moves away he begins to pat himself to make sure he still had what he had when his cousin embraced him. You can only be politically correct for so long. The church is not in the PC business. We are in the transformative business. We are in the business of changing the hearts of folks—not so they act right but so they be right. Because

[*] This sermon was preached at the forty-third annual meeting of National Black Methodists for Church Renewal held in 2010 in Jacksonville, Florida. View the preaching of this sermon on www.garrett.edu/styberg-bump/swanson

so much is going on that cries out for the church to be its best and to be what God intends for us to be.

Most of you are Bible scholars of some sort, and so I know you have learned that this letter that we call the Letter to the Ephesians, was not intended for the church at Ephesus. Indeed, it was kind of a letter that was supposed to be circulated to many churches and to be read as a sermon, a presentation, about what Paul believed the church ought to be—namely, a place of unity and harmony. Paul was concerned in particular with Jewish Christians learning how to be in fellowship with Gentile Christians, and with Gentiles knowing that they have been fully embraced and accepted by their Jewish brothers and sisters. So Paul in this letter sends it out to try and help the churches to understand that God is indeed calling us to a place of unity and harmony where we do not count someone higher than someone else because of their heritage or what they have or what they even might know. Instead, they are to accept that they are known and embraced and loved by God through Jesus Christ.

If you read this epistle you begin to catch some of Paul's excitement. In fact, the scripture I read again for you, if you look you will see that it contains a lot of commas. Back in my elementary days, when I was in grammar school, my teacher would have called it a run-on sentence and would have said add some periods. But I believe Paul had the spirit of Black preachers. Somehow we don't know how to stop. We start preaching and it gets good to us and we run past the periods and the exclamation points and we don't know when to pause except to take a breath of air and take off and run one more time. You can just see it here. Paul is excited about this presentation, about this sermon. He's trying to help people to understand we are called to be in unity and harmony with one another. Something that Paul says here, however, at the end of this fourth chapter that really intrigues me and fascinates me is that each of us been called and set aside for representative ministry. Understand that you are not your own. You don't belong to yourself.

I realize that we come into ministry with great expectations. It doesn't take long for a lay leader to let you know that your expectations do not meet reality. And sometimes we come in thinking that the whole world has been waiting for us. Sort of like back in the day they gave an A. B. degree and now they give a B. A. degree.

A man walks across the stage as he gets his paper and he shouts, "Look out, world, I got A. B." and he hears, "Sit down, son, and we will teach you the rest of the alphabet." We need to understand that here Paul is saying of being in representative ministry, it's a gift, and you yourself are that gift. And since you are a gift you cannot dictate to the giver how you are to be used. You are the gift. And because of that there is a particular purpose for you to fulfill and that is "to equip the saints for the work of ministry."

Now I recognize that does not always fit our mode. Because for some of us, we do have difficulty with accepting the fact that the laity are co-partners, partners with us in ministry. They are, in fact, when I look at it, like lamb and shepherd, sheep and shepherd. The shepherd has got his job: he's got to find his green pastures. And if you have ever been in the Holy Land you know it's not an easy job. You know those pictures you all have been seeing—I hope you all really go down there. Those pictures you've been seeing with Jesus, holding the lamb and the sheep lying all around his feet and green grass everywhere: whoever painted that has not been to the Holy Land. You go to the Holy Land and grass is sparse. It is hard to find grass, and the shepherd has got to look long and hard to find grass for the sheep to graze upon. It is not an easy job to be a shepherd. You have to climb over rocks, mountainsides, hang off the sides of them so you can find green grass for the sheep to eat. Not an easy job.

I don't know who fooled you into thinking when you got a Masters of Divinity that you were going to go somewhere and sit on the flower beds of ease and folks were going to bow down to you and all that kind of stuff. This is a hard job. And the reason I compare it to shepherd and sheep is because they are dependent on each other. The poor sheep can't even drink water unless the shepherd finds water that is not turbulent. It has to be still water. You all understand that. How much shoutin' goes on in your church when hell is being raised? When everybody is marching in front of the PPR committee (Pastor Parish Relations), saying, "get rid of you," I don't know how you all preach in those kinds of conditions—let alone how sheep are going to drink water when that is going on. Those folk need the shepherd.

Lay folk, you all need to understand, you do need a preacher. You need somebody who will tell you that you need to be transformed, that you need to be renewed, that you need to change. You need somebody to tell you that, and then you need to pay them for telling you! You need a shepherd, because you need someone who can protect you. I am not talking about hirelings. I am talking about shepherds. I'm talking about people who are committed; and at the same time, shepherds, you need sheep who will sacrifice their wool so that you might be warm in winter time, who allow you to take milk from them when it might nourish their own body and even when your food supply is running out they offer themselves to be slaughtered so that you and your families might eat. We need each other. We are in it together. So Paul is trying to help us understand the synergy that must exist in the church if we are to lead people in the way God wants the church to go.

Part of the problem, or perhaps I should say, the challenge that we face is that often times the church is guilty of settling for mediocrity, for just getting by, just limping along the journey. We are not really interested in becoming and being the best that we can be. Not at all. That's why I love Jim Collins's book *Good to Great*. He says, "Good is the enemy of great." That is one of the key reasons why we have so little that becomes great. You don't have enough great schools principally because we have good schools. We don't have great government principally because we have good government, despite what some folks say. Few people attain great lives because it is just so easy to settle down and nestle in with good. He's talking about the vast majority of companies precisely because the vast majority become quite good and that is their main problem.

And I want to say to Black Methodists for Church Renewal that we have to stop trying to be a good caucus. We've got to start understanding that we need to be a great caucus. We need to stop meddling with the little stuff that doesn't upset anybody. We have to be a great caucus. We have to understand that the goal is not being good or getting higher. The goal is perfection. As Paul says, "Until we all come to the maturity of faith of Jesus Christ, who is the head of the church." In other words it doesn't matter how far we've come, I still see Jesus on the horizon beckoning us to go one step further. And when we get there, Jesus is still ten steps ahead of us. He is pushing us to move further and further and to break barriers that we never have broken before, to do things in ways we never have done them before.

Oh, how far God has brought us. We are saying we want young folk in the church, and we are still dragging amazing grace. We are still afraid of the drums and tambourines; we are still afraid of the exuberance of young folks. When you get older you can't do what you used to do: you need to make room. God is trying to do a new thing among us. Folks don't want to hear us talk about miracles. They want to see miracles. They don't want us to talk about what it used to be like; they want to see what it can be today. They don't want us to talk about how many churches we used to have; they want to see more churches today. We should never be satisfied with how far we have come because we have not come as far as God wants us to become.

We have not because when we are at our best then violence will not only cease in the world but it will cease in some of our homes. Our young folk will quit dropping out of school and will get not only Master's but Ph.D. degrees. When we are at our best, our church will quit fussing over what color the wall is and do what makes God happy in the church. When we are at our best, we will say, "All to thee I surrender, all to thee I freely give." When we are at our best, we will see the sick recover. When we are at our best, we will see folk come running, saying, "I yield, I yield. I can't hold out much longer." When we are at our best, we will come to this table with humility in our hearts and we will know that he died for us.

We are not doing God a favor by showing up at the table. He did us the greatest thing that could ever happen. He went up a rugged hill and he carried that cross. They hung him high and stretched him wide from the sixth to the ninth hour. His head fell upon his breast. He gave up the ghost, and they partied all Friday night, Saturday morning, Saturday afternoon, and Saturday night. Sunday morning he got up, with all power in his hands. If you want to be the best, you have to work at it. You have to quit settling for mediocrity and know that the God we serve has called us to be the head and not the tail. God has called us to and through Jesus Christ so we can be the church at its best.

Give God the praise.

Conclusion

Gennifer Benjamin Brooks

On each occasion of preaching the goal is always to offer, one more time, the gift of divine grace that is good news of Christ's redeeming love. On the many, many occasions that I was privileged to sit at the feet of my mentor (if only for a few short years) and friend Bishop Edsel Ammons, he would say to me, sometimes in bewilderment, often in irritation at the shenanigans being performed in the pulpit by some preachers, "What is the matter with them? What is the church coming to with so-called preachers like that?" His love for the church and his respect for good preaching had little tolerance for persons and actions that did not take seriously the work of preaching that he considered critical to the life of the church. Bishop Ammons believed that quality preaching strengthened the church, and his prayer was always that pastors would take this task seriously.

In the few sermons that have been presented here are styles of preaching and shapes of sermons that are as varied as the preachers and my hope is that even reading them might help current and would-be preachers experience the grace of God that is represented in each one. It was important for me to allow each preacher to bring her or his genuine preaching voice into the conversation, so there were no instructions given as to the style of sermon that each should bring to the table. The only requirement was authenticity in their practice of the art, so that we might experience, even if only in a glimpse, the range of preaching styles that represents Black preaching.

The sermons are long and short, topical and expository, delivered with ease and with fire, and all offer a word from God that starts from scripture. Dependence on scripture is considered one of the main criteria of Black preaching, and these sermons are truly representative of Black preaching in all its glory. An additional feature of these sermons is that they have been preached in congregational settings and not simply written for reading. God gives each person a voice to be used to the glory of God. God gives each preacher a word to be delivered authentically so that the people of

God receive the good news of God's redeeming, empowering grace. Beyond the outer trappings of pastoral identity, homiletical integrity, biblical accuracy, poetic literacy, or energetic delivery, the preacher must be diligent so that the preached message will offer to the people the same gift of divine grace that empowered the preacher in the creation of the sermon.

It is imperative for both preacher and people that, despite personality, individual gifts of delivery, and style, all persons, preacher and people, hear the good news and thereby receive strength for the Christian journey. All people need the assurance that God's grace is available to them for the living of their days. All people who strive to live a life of truth and righteousness need the grace of God to sanctify their lives so that they might achieve the perfection in love that our Wesleyan heritage assures us is possible in this lifetime. And the whole people of God need to experience the good news as a present reality in their own lives and to experience the transformative grace it offers, enabling them to live as disciples of Jesus Christ. The task of the preacher is to assist the hearers to be kingdom dwellers in the present even as they strive to attain the goal of the future realm of God. In this endeavor, the preacher struggles alongside the people and seeks the unending grace of God for her or his life as disciple and preacher.

None of us, preacher or hearer, has yet arrived. We have a long way to go, but the goal remains as it ever was: eternity with Christ. In preaching, the goal is also the same as it ever was: to proclaim good news and point hearers to Christ. Bishop Ammons expressed the hope that his preaching always had done that, even if only for one soul. Approbation of the hearers can be seductive, and the preacher's commitment to the craft cannot be dependent on fleeting words of commendation. By focusing on Christ and seeking the anointing of the Holy Spirit, the preacher can be assured that God will give life to the words of the sermon so that they are transformed into the word of God. As you read the sermons presented here and perhaps listen to them as well, may they move you to examine your own preaching; may they help inspire you and move you to recommit yourself to faithfully offer the good news of God's redeeming love to the whole people of God.

It is my privilege and joy to offer this final sermon in recognition of Bishop Ammons's ministry as a preeminent preacher of the gospel. The sermon was preached in his presence at a celebration of his visionary leadership at Garrett-Evangelical Theological Seminary (G-ETS), which resulted in the creation of the Center for the Church and the Black Experience (CBE), now in its forty-first year of ministry at the seminary. Given his interest in the subject, his directives, and his support for the project, it seems only fitting that the final sermon be a tribute to this erudite, engaging, God-blessed, and Spirit-filled preacher of the church.

Miles to Go: Still the Same Goal*
Philippians 3:12-21

It was 1974 and I had just got my driver's license. I was young and adventurous (to put it mildly). I wasn't aware as yet that I am directionally challenged, so I set out for Toronto, Canada, to visit my sister with my nine-year-old niece and my five-year-old nephew in the car. I had gone to the Exxon center and I had maps marked with the route. I was ready. I don't think that I knew how long the trip was supposed to be, but I was ready. I had a goal, and I had directions. I set out at about 2:00 p.m. and I figured I would get there before midnight, and since I'm a night person, everything was in order. At 4:00 p.m., I was still about five minutes away from my home because I could not find the entrance to the highway. Finally, I found it, and I was on my way. Well, there are too many bridges in New York, and I couldn't understand the signs anyway, so at 6:00 p.m. I was just getting on to the New York State Thruway. But we were on the way. It was the Memorial Day weekend, and the traffic was heavy and some of it was slow-going, but I kept driving, and finally, there it was—The Peace Bridge. That was the bridge I had to cross and I would have arrived. We had been on the road for about ten hours by that time, but there it was—Canada. We began to celebrate; the end was in sight. We showed our passports, and we began to cross the bridge. We could barely hold our excitement—we had made it. There was the sign—Welcome to Canada. We were screaming with joy. And then we saw it, right in front of us—the next sign read: Toronto 120 miles. My niece said—no, she wailed—Aunt Gennifer. And the celebration ended: miles to go—many, many miles to go.

Paul is writing from prison in Rome and possibly, as many scholars believe, dealing with a major problem of disunity in the church—a problem that continues to plague us still today. But then again, that might not be the issue, as other scholars argue, because Paul does not waste time on much of that. His focus is on encouraging the church that he started in Philippi—a congregation that

* This sermon was preached in the Chapel of the Unnamed Faithful of Garrett-Evangelical Theological Seminary in Evanston, Illinois, on October 22, 2009. View the preaching of this sermon on www.garrett.edu/styberg-bump/brooks

represented a significant moment in his ministry because it was a new arena of endeavor for the fledgling Christ movement. The Roman citizenry of Philippi and their cult of the emperor, their loyalty to the ruling class and the wealth it represented, as well as the multiple divinities beyond the emperor, all presented a great challenge to Paul's mission and goal of making disciples of Jesus Christ. But Paul had met the challenge and started a Christian community in that place, and his pastor's heart is concerned about them.

In prison, Paul knows of the struggle, the persecution that members of the Philippian church are experiencing, but he doesn't focus on the negative. Beyond calling two church sisters to agree—God bless the church sisters—Paul offers a word of encouragement to the congregation. This letter is not, as some early scholarship has tried to make it, a finite and authoritative statement about the two natures of Christ—his humanity and his divinity. It is not the last or best christological statement of the church.

Both Barth and Luther understood the pastoral nature of the text. Francis Watson, in his work on the interpretation of Philippians, quotes Luther, who says: "The chief purpose of this letter is to build up, to pluck down, and to destroy all wisdom and righteousness of the flesh." But as I tell my students, we are not dealing with the whole letter here; we are dealing with a particular text. It is the end of Paul's letter, and his call is not simply to action but it is to perseverance. Paul's intent, having looked back at his own situation and the situation of the Philippian church; having examined, considered, and analyzed where he and they had come from, is to call them to the stark and sobering realization that while he and they had come a long way, they had not yet reached their goal.

"I have a dream." Paul might have said these words. Listen again to Paul: "Not that I have already obtained this or have already reached the goal, but I press on to make it my own." What is the goal of which he spoke? Was it freedom from prison? His mission as an apostle and evangelist had been successful, so was it starting more congregations? Was it winning more disciples for Jesus Christ? Dr. Martin Luther King, Jr., laid out what he considered of significance for the goal of freedom: "I have a dream that one day this nation will rise up and live out the true meaning of its creed: 'We hold these truths to be self-evident, that all men are created equal.' " And the journey began, the way ahead was mapped out carefully, and progress was made; but there was persecution, and real freedom seemed always to be just that much further ahead. And just when it seemed (at least to some) that we had made it, the signpost appeared in the middle of the hallowed halls of Congress, and with it the sobering realization—miles to go; many, many miles to go.

Bishop Ammons in formulating the idea of CBE had a dream of something new and different, an irresistible and unimagined future for the sake of the gospel. It was a new arena of endeavor for the school, a significant moment in the life of the seminary. And the center in its early days seemed destined to reach its goal. But as with all of life there were setbacks, misdirections, missed opportunities, unanticipated challenges; and at times it seemed not only that the goal was receding into the distance but that the work itself had come to an end. But then, like Paul's letter, there came a word of encouragement. A new administration; a new voice raising the standard; a new president that looked at the goal, saw the signs, and called for revitalization and renewal; saw the signposts, recognized the needs, and stepped out in faith.

And as it starts the next leg of the race with a new director, CBE can do no better than to return to the original dream. All of us may have come to this moment with our own ideas of what CBE is or should be. What that idea is may be different for the president, for the CBE director, for the Board of Visitors, the seminary trustees, the development officer, the CBE faculty individually and collectively, for every faculty member, for the Garrett-Evangelical Black Seminarians, and for each person here, but there is a dream, an idea, a goal if you will that many of us, if not all of us, have in mind for CBE. But unless that dream is rooted in the goal that Paul reminds us is the one, the only one that is important for us as people of Christ individually and corporately, then it is doomed to remain unrealized.

Paul's goal, his dream if you will, was eternity with Christ—resurrection from death to life everlasting. It was his focus on that goal that enabled him to live fully, whatever he faced; to demonstrate his commitment to Christ and the freedom of spirit that gave him. That is or should be every Christian's goal, and in its corporate identity of social holiness, to use John Wesley's words, it must be the goal of CBE. Paul urges us to press on even when there are detours that lengthen the journey, even when the goal seems to recede further and further in the distance; when there are miles to go, press on.

Press on, CBE, because there is life ahead; CBE's goal as the baton is passed is not simply to develop a better program, a better center that attends to the needs of the few—no matter how great those needs may be—but to raise up the standard of Christ in a way that transcends race and ethnicity, church and society; to go beyond limited resources, even beyond change that we can live with to truth and justice that we cannot live without; to demonstrate the richness of Christ's presence in the work that we do and the witness that we offer in his name. The call of God is still to an irresistible and unimagined future, and while we may not always agree on the path to take, as Paul reminds us, "that too God will make clear to [us]" (Philippians 3:15 NIV).

And so we must press on. We've come this far by faith: that is as true for CBE as it was for our African American ancestors and as it must be for us. We've miles to go to reach the goal of resurrection and new life with Christ, and we press on because we belong to Christ. Paul says: "[I have not] reached the goal; but I press on to make it my own, because Christ Jesus has made me his own" (3:12). Christ has made us his own; we belong to Christ; our work is Christ's, and it is Christ who empowers us to do the work; to strive for the goal; to reach the goal. Christ alone empowers us to reach the goal.

That night at the Canadian border, I felt that I could just turn back. My logical mind knew that it was a further distance that I had come than what was ahead, but my spirit was at its lowest ebb. Yet I continued, and fourteen hours after I left my home in Brooklyn, my niece and nephew and I arrived at my sister's home in Toronto. We were weary but jubilant: we had made it. What a feeling that was; what a joy; what a celebration! And what a joy it will be when we become fully what God has called us to be. What a celebration it will be when CBE becomes fully what God needs it to be. So press on, CBE, press on! Yes there are miles ahead, but Christ is with you, and with Christ, through Christ, in Christ we can reach the goal. Press on! Press on, my sisters! Press on, my brothers! The journey is worth it; we belong to Christ, and Christ is our goal, so press on! Press on to the goal of life, resurrected life, eternal life through Jesus Christ our Lord.

CPSIA information can be obtained at www.ICGtesting.com
Printed in the USA
LVOW121008080212

267711LV00001B/6/P